"Many parents freak when their offspring begin to show the first signs of independence. But relax! Just as he did for parents of preschoolers, Pettit will navigate you safely through the 'tween' years. His strategy for success is backed with the latest research, practical tips, and winsome real-life stories."

—Jim Congdon
Senior pastor, Topeka Bible Church

"As a sandwiched parent with a teen, a tween, and a future tween, I enjoyed *Congratulations, You've Got Tweens!*, particularly Pettit's emphasis on authentic communication. I appreciated the book's balanced, practical approach to parenting today's tweens."

—Mary E. DeMuth
Author of *Ordinary Mom, Extraordinary God* and
Building the Christian Family You Never Had

"Full of practical help for parents of preteens, this book is a terrific investment, both for your tween and for you. Paul Pettit speaks out of his own experience to help readers understand and relate to their kids in an ever-changing youth culture."

—Sandra Glahn, ThM
Author and parent of a preteen

Congratulations, you've got tweens!

Preparing Your Child for Adolescence

Paul Pettit

Kregel
Publications

Congratulations, You've Got Tweens!: Preparing Your Child for Adolescence

© 2007 by Paul Pettit

Published by Kregel Publications, a division of Kregel, Inc., P.O. Box 2607, Grand Rapids, MI 49501.

ISBN 13: 978-0-8254-3474-7

Printed in the United States of America

07 08 09 10 11 / 5 4 3 2

Lovingly dedicated to
Edward and Rita Pettit
and
Don and Alice Boden

Contents

Introduction

Where Did My Child's Childhood Go?

- Julie is frustrated because her ten-year-old daughter, Amanda, spends most of her afternoons browsing the Internet and "chatting" on instant messenger.

- Robert is concerned about his eight-year-old son, Ryan, and his involvement in select soccer. Their team has played in six different cities the last six weekends.

- Rita enjoys dressing Roberta, her third grade daughter, in cute "little girl" outfits. But Roberta complains and says she wants to dress like the high school girls she sees in her neighborhood.

- The talk around school is that nine-year-old Kyle and eight-year-old Krissie are already "going steady," have exchanged expensive bracelets, and have even kissed at the mall. Kyle's mom isn't sure what to do.

- Ray wants to communicate from his heart with his young son, Will. But their talks never end up sounding right. So Ray often avoids important discussions and instead talks with Will about superficial subjects.

- Susan isn't sure if she should keep Toni, her eleven-year-old daughter, close by her side, carefully protecting her from the outside world; or allow her to venture out, explore life on her own, and take her own bumps and bruises.

- Edward wants his son, eight-year-old Raymond, to go hiking, camping, and fishing with him, but Raymond says he'd rather play video games in his room.

Welcome to the wonderful and wonder-filled world of parenting tweens!

A word of caution here at the outset: There's no such thing as a perfect parent, perfect parenting, or a perfect tween. There's a rumor floating around stating you can be all things to your children—meet all of their needs and enjoy unbroken, intimate fellowship with your kids as they stumble through the normal developmental stages leading to adolescence.

If you buy into this myth and try to raise perfect children, you're setting up yourself and your children for big-time failure. Each of us is fatally flawed. Every one of us fails to reach the lofty, perfectionist standards we set for ourselves. We often fail several times in a single day! And ultimately we can't determine or even control the decisions our tweens end up making.

The opposite reaction to this perfect-parent myth is as extreme as trying to raise flawless kids. Sometimes we reason that, since our children are headed toward a wild, uncontrollable period called adolescence, the best we can do is to virtually remove ourselves from the equation, stick our heads in the sand, and hope for the best as our tweens somehow develop into teens on their own.

Since we know we're far from perfect, we sometimes allow this type of distorted thinking to de-emphasize the incredible importance of our role. We see our children growing, maturing, and developing, and we reason, *I guess I had my shot. I should have done more when they were younger!*

Okay now. Relax—take a long, deep breath. You're one out of the millions and millions of struggling, imperfect parents. All parents are, in fact, imperfect, raising imperfect children.

You can probably guess where I'm going with these two extremes of perfection and apathy. Neither is healthy. Fortunately, they aren't our only options for parenting a tween. While we can never become flawless parents, we can serve our children well as highly effective parents. We can learn to parent with purpose. We can study and practice the seasoned advice given by credentialed family researchers and veteran parents. Like playing the violin well, parenting requires practice.

The world grows ever more dangerous and daunting, so we shouldn't sit in our bedrooms and twiddle our thumbs while our kids flounder on their own. Nor should we grab our children and retreat to a backwoods encampment for anxious and frightened parents. You know the place—all scissors are confiscated and kids aren't allowed into the swimming pool until one hour after they've eaten!

In Be-*tween*

What should we do, then, to avoid these two parenting extremes? In order to determine what unique strategy to take with your child (because every child is unique), you must first define where your child is developmentally.

> ### Definitions
> *Puberty* refers to the process of physical changes by which a child's body becomes an adult body capable of reproduction.[1]
>
> *Adolescence* is the period of psychological and social transition between childhood and adulthood.[2]

You already know that your child is no longer an infant. He no longer needs diapers, bouncy seats, or "onesies." Bicycles and electric scooters have replaced the strollers and tricycles of his toddler years. But, despite what your child may think, your eight- to twelve-year-old is not yet an adolescent, let alone an adult.

She's living be-*tween* (hence the name) the earlier developmental stages of learning to talk, walk, and chew, and is moving toward the stage of more complex and difficult emotional and psychological growth. She's determining that she is her own "person" apart from her family of origin. She's beginning to form her own values, goals, and beliefs.

All of the physical and emotional changes your child encounters during these periods of rapid development end up affecting you as well as your child. My guess is that your original, clear vision for parenting effectively with purpose is becoming partly cloudy to downright foggy.

Successfully navigating this stage of your child's maturation is, while not easy, vital to who he will become as an adult. It is highly critical you walk *with* your child through these important days of development.

Ponder for a moment this question: When your son or daughter is thirty or forty years old, will the two of you be close? Will the two of you enjoy a healthy adult-to-adult relationship?

The fact is that you and your tween are headed for an emotional *break*. This break will not happen in one instant but will proceed slowly during the tween years.

During this sensitive time, your tween has an assignment she must perform. She needs to form and fashion her unique self-identity—separate from yours. It's critical that your tween develops a healthy self-image, a positive picture of who she is. Your tween needs to know and believe she is capable of accomplishing her upcoming task of living life on her own as an adult.

This period of adjustment can sometimes be rocky. The good news, however, is that after this uncertain period of *leaving* occurs, a beautiful period of *uniting* ensues. The leaving stage, in fact, sets up and makes possible the uniting stage—in which the two of you are no longer interacting as parent to child but as friend to friend.

Your relationship must change. You can't remain the constant caregiver. At points during your tween's development, he needs to

Physical Changes of Puberty in Girls

- Breast development: A firm, tender lump appears under the center of the areola of one or both breasts, occurring on average at about 10.5 years.
- Menstruation: The average age for the first signs of menstrual bleeding is 12.7 years. Menstrual periods are not always regular or monthly in the first 1–2 years.
- In response to rising levels of estrogen, the lower half of the pelvis widens and fat tissue increases to a greater percentage of the body composition than in males, especially in the breasts, hips, and thighs. This produces the typical female body shape.
- Another effect of puberty is increased secretion of oil (sebum) from the skin and the appearance of acne, which varies greatly in severity.

Physical Changes of Puberty in Boys

- Testicular enlargement (11.5 years) is the first physical manifestation of puberty.
- Within months after growth of the testes begins, rising levels of testosterone promote growth of the penis, scrotum, and pubic hair.
- Adult height is reached at an average of 17.5 years.
- Increased levels of androgens cause the male voice to drop about one octave. In the early stages, voice change is occasionally accompanied by cracking and breaking sounds.

> ## Baseline Shift in the Onset of Puberty
>
> * The age at which puberty occurs has dropped significantly since the 1840s.
> * From 1840 through 1950 a drop of four months per decade occurred in the average age of the onset of puberty among Western European females. Whereas today the onset age of puberty for girls is 10.5, in 1840 the average age was 16.5.[3]

envision what it will be like for him to live on his own. The upcoming pages will explore how you and your child can arrive at this beautifully harmonious place together.

Parenting is your responsibility. Parenting *well*, however, is your choice. We could actually call parenting well our spiritual service of worship. Parenting effectively can serve as a sacrificial offering to God. He has given our children to us as gifts—we are stewards of their development.

In a real sense, our tweenage children are on loan to us from God. The very fact that we have children is God's gift to us. The manner and style in which we parent our children is our gift to God.

Taking Action

As a parent of tweens, I know that talking and even writing about good parenting is easier than actually pulling it off. I'm a realist when it comes to parenting. My father was an elementary school principal and my mother was a substitute school teacher. I served as a youth pastor for four years. I've worked with hundreds of students in my current role as a graduate school administrator. Believe me—I've heard countless stories of both good and bad parenting.

The purpose of this book, then, is not only to encourage you in your parenting efforts but also to *equip* you for the special task of parenting tweens. This book presents practical tips that work for parenting preadolescents, and describes the ongoing developmental processes that impact both you and your maturing child.

The more specific purpose of this book is to suggest two powerful parenting strategies you can use to make the normal child-to-adolescent transition a healthy and smooth one. Currently, your child is emotionally swinging between (1) feeling loved, nurtured, and secure in the warmth of the family nest, and (2) mentally and emotionally preparing to leave the safety of your home and venturing forth into the scary world to explore life on her own.

So the first strategy involves practicing what I call *balanced parenting*—that is, avoiding the extremes of either harsh rule-setting or disengagement—when interacting with your child. The second strategy involves employing *authentic communication*—or being honest and open with your child and speaking the truth in love—as your foundation for parent/child discussions. Throughout this book, these two parenting strategies will be thoroughly explained and illustrated.

Also included are helpful hints, real-life stories from my own parenting experience of raising five kids, current results from academic research, and sage advice from seasoned parents who've served serious time in the parenting trenches. In addition, you can evaluate several case studies presented with discussion questions so you can *see* how these strategies take place. These case studies and discussion questions work extremely well in small group settings; you can use them, however, in whatever situation you choose.

Similar Parenting Systems

The two vital parenting practices described in this book—balanced parenting and authentic communication—demonstrate a pattern of proven results. Several recent approaches to effective parenting are, in fact, similar and share this give-and-take, love-and-limits approach.

Dr. Cynthia Neal Kimball, assistant professor of psychology at Wheaton College, teaches a form of "modeling after the parents." In this model, authority slowly shifts over time from the parents to the child. Kimball employs a construction metaphor and has labeled her approach *scaffolding*. Imagine a tall building being constructed in your town. First, the builders place a scaffold around and along the first floor as the foundation is poured. Next the scaffold is raised as the first floor is completed and work on the second floor commences. When the building is complete, the scaffolding is removed. You get the picture. In the parenting process, scaffolding represents the close boundaries provided by parents as tweens mature and take on more responsibility for their actions. When parents feel their teens are ready, they gradually remove those boundaries.

Dr. Kimball states,

> Scaffolding is a form of nurture and guidance that allows the center of regulation to shift gradually and appropriately from the nurturer to the child. The process requires considerable attention and sensitivity on the part of the nurturer, who must discern when the child needs support in the forms of actual help, modeling behavior, verbal instruction, emotional safety, or demonstrated approval, and when the child is to be left to his or her own devices in these respects.[4]

Another balanced-parenting champion, Dr. Tim Kimmel, advocates a *grace-based* parenting approach. He, too, encourages a healthy balance, which includes both rule setting and relationship building. From his years of work with Christian families he knows all too well how quickly rules without relationship leads to rebellion. He summarizes God's parenting approach by noting,

> I'm urging you to raise your children the way God raises His. The primary word that defines how God deals with His children is grace. Grace does not exclude obedience, respect, boundaries, or discipline, but it does determine the climate in

which these important parts of parenting are carried out. You may be weird and quirky, but God loves you through His grace with all of your weirdness and quirkiness.[5]

The emphasis in the approach advocated in this book, similarly, centers upon you as parents learning to fully release your children. It's one thing to build a relationship with your tween, or to dismantle the boundaries around your tween. It's another thing to release your child, and not merely let him go, but over time to encourage him to become released from you as you sense he is undertaking and fully owning responsibility for his own actions.

When you're parenting your tween well, it feels like you're holding a fledgling dove in your hand. You keep your hands clasped tightly enough so that you won't drop the dove before it can fly on its own, but you don't squeeze so hard that you end up smothering the dove. It feels like you're holding the fledgling in a way that the dove can move and breathe without being crushed. It also feels like you're hands are steady, providing a firm platform from which the fledgling will eventually take flight. Remember, you're not raising a child—you're raising a future adult.

So whether you refer to a healthy, balanced parenting style as scaffolding, grace-based, or another term, the emphasis lies in avoiding harsh extremes.

This book is offered, then, not only to provide sound parenting advice, but to support and applaud you along your incredible journey. I enjoy encouraging parents. In fact, it's the reason I'm so excited about this particular volume you're holding. Since parenting tweens requires an enormous investment of time and energy, I'm guessing you could use a healthy dose of vitamin E (encouragement) right about now.

Here's your first dose. The facts show you can make an incredibly positive impact on your children. Read the following list of research nuggets thoughtfully and slowly. Think about your child and your parenting style as you scan these findings.

- Strong attachment relationships formed early in life between children and their parents promote in the child a sense of trust and confidence in others throughout the child's lifespan.

- Individuals whose childhood experiences with their parents were consistently characterized by warmth, care, and predictability had higher quality peer relationships and more positive emotional adjustment.

- Children who have strong attachments with their parents express greater emotional well-being and are less likely to engage in risk-taking behaviors such as crime, vandalism, and drug and alcohol abuse.[6]

Your child and your parenting style are unique. So I always encourage parents to seek advice and direction from a wide variety of credible sources. I believe, however, that the Bible is the very best source of wisdom for parenting. The idea of family is, after all, God's idea. I've devoted much of my life to studying Scripture at the highest academic levels. Because I believe in the core applicability of the Bible, all of the parenting advice I offer is solidly based on Scripture and is applied primarily to the culture in which we live and move and raise our tweens.

I urge you to stay the course while delving into this book and practicing the applications found within. Raise your sights. Look past recent mistakes and yesterdays failings, and dream with me about tomorrow's opportunities. Visualize your daughter receiving her high school diploma, learning to drive a car, voting for the first time. Visualize your son becoming all that the Creator designed him to be.

You can do it. You can raise a healthy young person who becomes a valuable, contributing member of the society called productive adults. Allowing God to work in you and through you to "bring up a child" is one of the most thrilling challenges of adulthood. Sure it's hard work, but the results will greatly impact your community and live on for generations to come.

1

The Need for Balanced Parenting

This Chapter's Big Idea

God exists relationally in authentic community. This is how we are to live as well. We first learn to live relationally as dependent children within the structure and safety of loving families. Healthy children are balanced children who develop and mature into the period called adolescence by slowly *individuating* and *separating* emotionally from their families of origin. This natural break begins developmentally between the ages of eight and twelve.

During this period of self-discovery, your tween will likely be searching, testing, and experimenting. He'll wonder if his interests lie in sports or music. He'll wonder if he'd rather draw pictures of race cars or the family pets. It's your opportunity to help your tween navigate through all the choices this life offers.

Balanced parenting, then, produces a balanced child who we hope is healthy not only in body, but in mind and spirit as well. If this sounds overwhelming, take heart. You're not alone. You have help in the form of community—or communities—that can act as your support system.

First Steps

A friend of mine recently told me of watching his daughter, Bryanna, learn to walk. At first his toddler took tentative steps, clinging to my friend and a trusty blue couch in the living room.

Bryanna's little legs would wobble and shake as she peered wide-eyed over her shoulder at the family dog and well-worn toys lying just out of reach. She'd let go with one hand but then quickly reach back for support. It wasn't long, however, before Bryanna was letting go of her dad's hand, pushing away from the couch, and taking her first independent steps. My friend was super excited that his very own daughter was beginning to *really* walk!

I smiled at the familiar excitement, and acknowledged that kids really don't walk—and later run—until they do it *independently*. Yes, they fall—we hope on their backsides and not their faces. Sure, they'll likely end up with bruises and maybe even a split lip. But you and I know those bumps and bruises are necessary steps for our children's learning to walk alone.

Emphasized throughout this book is the idea that children often repeat similar uncomfortable cycles as they mature. And the sometimes painful process of arriving at postadolescent independence is one of those cycles. Just like stumbling toddlers eagerly learning to walk, your anxious tween will need ongoing support while slowly learning what it fully means to be an independent adolescent moving toward adulthood. But your tween can't become that person without letting go . . . of you . . . and getting a few bumps and bruises in the process.

Steps Toward Independence

The bottom line is, your tween must learn to emotionally separate from you. The physical separation will come later, toward the conclusion of the teen years. But the emotional separation must take place before the physical. This emotional requirement of letting go isn't easy, but it's necessary and normal.

Infants must feel securely attached to their primary caregivers. This *secure base* allows for healthy self-exploration. Older children must also feel securely attached to their primary caregiver, which also leads to healthy self-exploration.

Preadolescents, however, must begin to move away from attachment relationships with parents and other authority figures. This is a normal and natural step for tweens. Secure attachment-bonds between authority figures and preadolescents are often viewed by tweens as ties that bind instead of secure bases that allow for healthy exploration.[1]

Remember, a key developmental task children must undertake as they enter into adolescence is to search out and develop autonomy. *Autonomy* is an interesting word. The root, *nomos,* means "law," and the prefix *auto* means "self." So what a tween is searching for is a way to govern the self apart from authority figures who impose law. In a real sense tweens rebel against the various authority figures in their lives because they're struggling with how to find ways to govern themselves. Your tween is searching for ways to write his individual life script—his unique laws of life.

Rebellion in the life of the tween, then, is not always unhealthy but can be normal and natural. We can't, of course, allow a tween or teen who's searching for autonomy to break established rules and regulations of school, family, or society. There must always be limits present as well as love in abundance. But the fact remains that tweens, by their very job description, are searching for ways to make new rules for themselves.

Tweens *must* develop autonomy so that they are no longer forced to rely on their parents for every life decision. (*"Hey, which jeans are you going to wear today?" "I don't know. My mom hasn't told me yet."*) This necessity is one of the reasons tweens flee to friends so quickly during this developmental period and form such strong attachments with peers.

Tweens are continually searching for their own unique identity, apart from that of their parents, and their friends have embarked upon a similar quest. This task unites tweens and bonds them together as they question their parents' authority and search for their own rules and regulations by which they believe they should live. It's no wonder tweens and teens who are searching for their new identities so identify with the slogan, "Question Authority."

While there are no magic formulas for successful parenting and no identical kids, there are basic ideas that can help your tween—and you—through this period of emotional separation. These ideas center around gender differences; balanced, "whole person" development; and the communities that are necessary in providing your child with the best support available.

> ### Girls Suffer from
> ### Negative Body Image
> Dieting has now become a common behavior for girls as young as age ten. One nutrition researcher believes dieting among tween girls should be reason for concern because of growth, fatigue, irritability, low self-esteem, depression, and eating disorder issues. More than 25 percent of girls in one study agreed with the statement, "Pictures of thin girls and women make me wish I were thin," and "I wish I looked like a magazine model."[2]

Gender Differences

A growing body of evidence in the literature produced by family studies researchers suggests important differences in the ways boys and girls develop into healthy teenagers. One stand out difference, for example, is the manner in which tweens make and maintain friendships. This may only serve to confirm what you have long suspected, but one study found that "there is evidence in the friendship literature to suggest that girls may have more intimate relationships with their friends than boys do and that girls may be more strongly affected than boys by the tensions and strains in their best friendships than boys are."[3]

Research also suggests that masculinity and femininity play an important role in the processes of individuation and separation. A fascinating study on these gender differences points out that

Traditionally, autonomy, independence, agency, and individuation have been associated with masculinity; interdependence, communion, and relationality have been associated with femininity . . . because the development of masculinity requires separation from the mother, boys and men define themselves in terms of separation and individuation. On the other hand, because girls tend to be parented by a person of the same gender, femininity is defined through attachment and relatedness.[4]

A girl, then, may feel more of a need to stay attached to her best friends and to you as a parent for a longer period and in a closer relationship than a son. This should not be cause for concern.

Boys may feel a stronger need to separate from you more quickly and more deeply than do girls. And this, too, should not cause undue alarm. A girl can remain attached to her mother and father in a close emotional and physical bond while continuing to mature in her femininity. This closeness is normal and healthy.

Girls who stay emotionally attached into adulthood, however, without being required to explore a healthy type of separation are sometimes demonstrating signs of unhealthy attachment and are referred to derogatorily as a "daddy's girl." That is to say, *That girl cannot succeed at anything unless her daddy does everything for her.*

Research proves that a boy, on the other hand, needs to make an emotional and physical break from his mother in order to explore his own budding masculinity, which his mother does not possess. Scholars refer to this extra step in healthy gender development as *the male problematic.*

It is labeled a problem because some boys never make the break from the otherwise healthy feminine influence the mother provides. Thus, they never fully develop functionally in their own masculinity. These boys go into the postadolescent period still feeling fully attached to their mothers and unattached to older male or father figures.

Boys who stay securely emotionally attached to their mothers into young adulthood without being required to explore a healthy type of separation are sometimes referred to derogatorily as a "mama's boy," or as a boy who is still attached to his mom's apron strings.

> ## The Importance of Gender Identity
> Leading family researcher Dr. Joseph Nicolosi reports that homosexuality is an identity problem. He says, "At the root of almost every case of homosexuality is some distortion of the fundamental concept of gender. . . . Self-deception about gender is at the heart of the homosexual condition. A child who imagines that he or she can be the opposite sex—or be both sexes—is holding on to a fantasy solution to his or her confusion. This is a revolt against reality and a rebellion against the limits built into our created human natures." In addition, Dr. Nicolosi states that gender identity is established very early within the context of the family.[5]

Single Parents

One of the frequent questions I'm asked on radio and television talk shows relates to children raised in single-parent homes. How are these children, it is often asked, supposed to develop healthy gender identities when they are living with only one parent? There's no simple answer to this question. One key, however, lies in the biblical idea of healthy community.

Children in single-parent homes must be surrounded with loving extended family members and healthy authoritative communities. A tween girl with no mother-model in her life needs to spend both quality and quantity time with a loving aunt or grandmother. If neither of these is available, then the faith community should be the next concentric circle in which to seek out a feminine role model.

If you're a single dad raising a daughter, is there a mature woman active in your place of worship who would commit to playing an involved role in the healthy gender development of your daughter? Pray that God will bring such a woman into your daughter's life, and then work hard to help this relationship flourish and develop.

If you're a single mom raising a son, allow your son to spend plenty of time with a healthy uncle or grandfather who can teach your boy what it means to be a man. If no such man exists, look in your faith community and pray that God brings such a man into your son's sphere of influence. A secure masculine influence is needed in addition to the feminine influence you provide.

Can you sense the explosive power of gender differences? Obviously extra parenting sensitivity toward these amazing, God-granted differences is needed. I don't believe a gender-neutral parenting style—that is, one under which no allowances are made for differences between boys and girls—is healthy. We should be prepared for a girl's real need for secure and prolonged attachment in the preteen years and a boy's healthy desire for separation. Special wisdom is needed in knowing when to encourage a girl's exploration of the outside world and when to reign in a boy's fight against domestication. Finding a balance between these extremes is required with both male and female tweens.

Praying for Future Marriage Partners

During the researching and writing of this book, I discussed gender development with several seasoned parents. They encouraged me to relay to you the importance of discussing and praying with your tween about the subject of a potential future marriage partner. Can you see what a powerful affirmation this can be for tweens who are struggling with their own developing sexuality?

There may be nothing more affirming for a young girl than to have her mother and father pray with her that God provide a tender, lifelong, loving husband. And the same goes for your son. You can greatly encourage your son's emerging masculinity by praying that God would graciously lead him to a faithful, caring, respectful wife.

Praying with your child is always a tremendous step of faith. It connects parent and child at both a physical level, as you may hold hands or place your arm around your tween's shoulders, for example, and a spiritual level, and also points the child toward a higher authority. By showing your tween that you willingly and gladly submit to a higher authority, it helps your child see that he should likewise submit to you as a parental authority.

Raising a "Whole Person"

In addition to gender differences, one of the most difficult challenges of raising tweens is their constant fluctuation between acting

Gender-healthy Children

Signs of healthy gender development arrive early in a child's life. In addition, unhealthy indicators of gender development also occur during the age range of four to eight. The American Psychiatric Association (APA) reports five danger signs of gender-identity disorder; that is, children behaving as and sometimes believing they are the opposite sex.

- Repeatedly stated desire to be or insistence that he or she is the other sex.
- In boys, preference for cross dressing or simulating female attire. In girls, insistence on wearing only stereotypical masculine clothing.
- Strong and persistent preference for cross-sexual roles in make-believe play, or persistent fantasies of being the other sex.
- Intense desire to participate in the stereotypical games and pastimes of the other sex.
- Strong preference for playmates of the other sex.[6]

like a child and straining to be considered by others as an adult. This seesaw pattern might leave you wondering which persona you'll encounter in your tween at any given moment. But this undulating experimentation is highly normal and also necessary for a child's growth. Your tween is experimenting with different confidence levels. One day she sees herself as a little child who craves the love and limits that only you can bring. The very next day she may believe she possesses the self-image of a graduate student studying for final exams.

The Chinese symbol for the word *crisis* includes the symbol for *danger* and the symbol for *opportunity*. When we witness our tweens trying on these vastly differing personas, we may consider this time period a crisis. But we should also view this time as one of great opportunity. It is during this time that we are increasingly able to exert a strong influence in what our children believe about themselves and their roles in the world.

Advice from Dr. Luke

The most trusted sources for advice about parenting are no longer readily available. World wars and the spread of industrialization separated many intact family units from supportive grandparents and other caring relatives. So baby boomer parents turned to the wisdom and advice of Dr. Benjamin Spock. Dr. Spock's informed words filled the cultural void and helped educate and calm the fears of millions of disillusioned, lonely parents.

> The content disseminated by today's technology has ushered in premature adolescence, challenging parents and educators to deal with this difficult developmental stage before they are ready. Researchers found that by third grade, 15 percent of children worried that their parents didn't understand them.[7]

Today's parents are equally frustrated and in need of even more wise advice. A rapidly changing global economy and instant world-wide communication have quickened the pace of parenting. Today's children are being asked to mature at alarmingly fast rates—so much so that the eight- to twelve-year-olds of today are expected to possess the maturity level of yesterday's teens. Many of today's parents are so busy, so preoccupied with keeping up the frantic pace, that they hardly have time for balanced living, let alone balanced parenting.

Whereas your parents cried out for Dr. Spock, I believe you and your peers need an equally relevant doctor. Like most of your friends, you are probably well versed in caring for physical problems like chicken pox and measles. What you likely need is relevant advice that will help you raise well-rounded, wise children. The inspired words of Dr. Luke sound as fresh today as when they were first recorded.

Dr. Luke, who traveled with the apostle Paul, was a physician. In all four of the gospels, very little is recorded regarding the childhood of Jesus. Luke records in his gospel, however, that before Jesus was twelve, the young boy grew and became strong, was filled with wisdom, and the grace of God was upon him (Luke 2:40). It's as though Dr. Luke, through his narrative, has provided for us the results of a checkup on the boy Jesus.

By using the terms "grew and became strong" (NIV), Dr. Luke is reporting that the process of Jesus' physical maturity was right on track. While we can only speculate, we can assume Jesus associated with other children his age,[8] learned to obey his parents, and began to learn and practice the trade of his earthly father, Joseph. By his display of the intricacies of Old Testament knowledge, we can postulate that Jesus was schooled by his parents and teachers in the history and ways of his people, the Jews.[9]

So we learn from Dr. Luke's report that by the age of twelve, Jesus was maturing in all four of the critical developmental categories of loving the Lord God with all of the (1) heart, (2) soul, (3) strength, and (4) mind (NIV).[10] This fourfold template of the balanced child can also be used in evaluating our parenting efforts.

Finding the Right Balance

Balanced parenting, which helps us raise healthy, well-adjusted children, requires our taking a close look at each of these four areas in the lives of our tweens—where they stand emotionally, spiritually, physically, and mentally. Our children ought to be maturing in all of these areas. At the same time, we need to keep central that each child is an amazingly unique gift from God and matures at a unique and individual rate. Your child is one of a kind, formed in the womb by the Creator of the universe. You'll need to trust he knows what he's doing.

You must keep a discerning eye on the "whole" of your child's development. If your tween shows talent or interest in a particular area, encourage him. You'll also want to watch for overbearing coaches or teachers who might push your son, or you, hard in one area. Some well-meaning friends or teachers push our kids so hard in one area that development in other areas is negatively affected.

I urge you to follow the balanced parenting approach whereby the child feels free to discover and develop her strengths and passions (*Basketball is awesome!*) yet is disciplined enough to tackle the difficult realities of living in the real world (*If I don't take out the trash and feed the dog I won't receive my allowance!*).

Many people have recognized the need for developing the whole person. During the American Industrial Revolution, children and parents were separated during long periods of the day by difficult work conditions. This familial separation caused an obvious deterioration in the development of children. So it wasn't simply chance that by the turn of the century numerous organizations and ministries were formed to meet a crucial family need.

In 1866, for example, the influential New York YMCA (Young Men's Christian Association) adopted a fourfold purpose statement:

"The improvement of the spiritual, mental, social, and physical condition of young men."[11] Another group calling itself 4-H was started in 1898. The four H's stand for Head, Heart, Hands, and Health. They are the four ongoing values the members work on through the 4-H's various programs.[12]

The following Scripture passages also expand on the heart, soul, strength, and mind concept, highlighting the whole-person developmental approach:

> I shall pray with the spirit and I shall pray with the mind also; I shall sing with the spirit and I shall sing with the mind also. (1 Cor. 14:15)

> Now may the God of peace Himself sanctify you entirely; and may your spirit and soul and body be preserved complete. (1 Thess. 5:23)

> For the word of God is living and active and sharper than any two-edged sword, and piercing as far as the division of soul and spirit, of both joints and marrow, and able to judge the thoughts and intentions of the heart. (Heb. 4:12)

Evangelical scholars emphasize the biblical idea of man's existing as a whole person—a unified, composite being with both material and immaterial aspects. These aspects are often labeled body and spirit. Whenever Jesus and the New Testament writers discussed the four parts of a human—heart, soul, strength, and mind—they emphasized that we are to love the Lord our God with our entire being. We are to serve God in everything we do.

The apostle Paul, for example, wrote to the Corinthians, "Whether, then, you eat or drink or *whatever you do,* do all to the glory of God" (1 Cor. 10:31, emphasis added). This is how we must view the outcomes and goals we set with and for our tweens.

I recently overheard a parent commenting on another child by saying, "She's not a very good student . . . but she's so spiritual!" And

I once heard a father announce, "I take my boy hunting, but I leave the spiritual stuff to his mom." These types of comments underscore an unbalanced approach to parenting and serve to highlight that some parents are missing major areas of their children's healthy development. We should strive to see our children develop in a balanced manner, with balance defining our role in our tweens' ongoing development. Balanced parenting requires continually looking out for the whole of our child's development.

It's your wonderful responsibility to help your tween develop into a whole person—to know where the balance lies between each necessary element of your child's life. This responsibility should weigh heavily on you, but it doesn't have to be difficult or a chore.

Say you sense your tween is stressed or struggling with a heavy load of academic work. Why not take a break, pull on your swimsuits, and head out to the driveway for a soaking, splashing time of washing the car? Or perhaps your tween looks bored and unchallenged. Take out a piece of paper and brainstorm some exciting goals the two of you desire to accomplish before the month is out. Or, if you sense your daughter is simply exhausted from one too many gymnastics lessons, why not encourage a week off with purposeful visits to a museum or art gallery? Once again, the objective is to strive for a balanced approach in your parenting, which often leads to a balanced tween.

One of my daughters and I recently attended a father/daughter summit. This one-day event provided an incredible context for sharing our goals and dreams with each other. To make sure we were being concrete with our plans, the leaders asked us to talk about one activity we desired to embark upon together once we returned home.

I promised my daughter we would go golfing together—just the two of us, without her brothers. I also added that she could drive the golf cart solo! (I'm normally the golf cart hog.) Some young daughters may not place "golfing with dad" at the top of their wish lists, but what young girl doesn't enjoy chasing after her golf-club wielding father with a speeding golf cart!

When it came time for my daughter to announce her desired activity, she asked that we—again, just the two of us, no brothers or sisters tagging along—go out for dinner at a really fancy restaurant (dads know that "fancy" is code speak for "expensive") where we would be required to dress up.

The activities you undertake with your tween may be vastly different—and less dangerous or expensive—than those just described. The point is that the outings are fun, meaningful, and that they help balance whatever other activities and stress your tween is facing.

Reducing "Screen Time" for Tweens

The Department of Health and Human Services Centers for Disease Control and Prevention (CDC) is worried about tweens and their "screen time." This lifestyle behavior leads to obesity in children and refers to the amount of time spent in a sedentary position, including watching television, playing video games, or using a computer. The average tween spends four-and-a-half hours each day in front of a screen.

- 26 percent of U.S. children watch four or more hours of television per day
- 67 percent of U.S. children watch two or more hours per day
- 48 percent of families with tweens have all four "media staples": TV, VCR, video game equipment, and a computer
- Of children 9–13 years old, 57 percent have TVs in their bedrooms[13]

Community

The Bible is very clear regarding the importance of community. Believers are urged to meet consistently together (Heb. 10:25). Jesus had his twelve disciples as well as a community (including Mary,

Martha, and Lazarus) with whom he consistently met. And older, mature women are asked to help model Christian womanhood for younger women (Titus 2:3–5). The idea of community is further evidenced in the relational description and theological explanation of who God is. He exists relationally in a "family" structure. The Father, Son, Spirit essence operates in perfect harmony and sinless perfection.

Although our human interactions never occur in a perfect environment, God's plan is that we live our lives in authentic community as he does. The family system gives tweens a place where they can learn to live under authority and in community.

From his incredible design template, it is God's unwavering desire that we first learn how to live in community within our family of origin. Then, as we grow and mature, he desires that we learn to live in healthy community as a member of the family of God. Many of the same lessons we learn from our own families inside our homes are also to be practiced within the family of God in our places of worship.

Further, we are to model healthy community in our neighborhoods, towns, and cities, and in the broader context of society with friends, coworkers, and neighbors. This developmental stage we might call "learning to live in community and under authority" is one of the first tests of preadolescence and eventually successful adulthood.

In addition, family researchers have found that it's important for tweens to learn to live in community because preadolescents must develop their own identity. And tweens do this by slowly separating from the identity of their parents and developing healthy, close relationships with their friends and others.[14]

In other words, tweens cannot join in authentic communities until they are able to clearly define who they are as individuals. One must possess a healthy sense of one's own identity before one can become a functioning, contributing member of a healthy community.

The isolated lamb is easy prey for the hungry wolf. The lone coal, separated from the bonfire, is quickly extinguished. Use whatever metaphor you wish—tweens in isolation are accidents waiting to happen. Our preadolescents need to be actively involved in a healthy community.

> ### Trouble Comes to Tweens
> In 1971, the age of juvenile delinquents was fifteen, sixteen, and seventeen years old. Today, troubled juveniles are tweens aged eight, nine, and ten. So says Dr. James McBreen, professor of social work at the University of Cincinnati. He warns, "One of the issues we are working with here is how do we help the community build a web of support for children? The kinds of communities we knew as kids, as neighborhoods, don't exist anymore for kids this age. The neighbor next door is not going to call your mom anymore and tell her if you've done something wrong. The idea of community is missing."[15]

Parents and Family

Dr. Luke also writes in his gospel that, "Jesus kept increasing in wisdom and stature, and in favor with God and men" (Luke 2:52). This descriptive update from the physician appears after the time frame when Jesus was twelve years old and before the beginning of Jesus' earthly ministry at his public baptism when he was thirty years old.

But the really amazing insight shared from Dr. Luke's developmental report is the brief mention of Jesus' relationship with his parents during this eighteen year period from ages twelve to thirty. Tucked away in verse fifty-one of chapter two is the brief notation that Jesus, while living with his parents, "continued in subjection to them."

Amazing! The perfect Son of God lived out his days as a developing preadolescent in humble subjection to his earthly, flawed parents. What a tremendous example. What an inspiration for you and your tweens. Children in the eight- to twelve-year-old range are certainly not yet mature enough to live in the world on their own. They've been given God-ordained guardians and protectors to look out for their best interests. No matter what our culture screams, today's tweens are to live "in subjection" to their parents just as Jesus did.

But as children begin to individuate and separate from the family of origin, they enter a stressful and awkward time. God has, in his providential wisdom, provided the caring environment of the family and the loving discipline of parents to help children mature and develop during this sensitive period. What better laboratory is possible for maturing children as they experiment with preadolescence? The home, with two healthy, loving adults is God's plan—and it's wonderful.

The ideal is a safe place where children know where they stand in relation to those in authority over them and yet also feel free to explore, discover, and become themselves. The brilliant Danish philosopher Søren Kierkegaard wrote, "And now, with God's help, I shall endeavor to become . . . myself."[16] As parents, we need to help our tweens become their best, most authentic selves.

Living in a Broken World

The ideal for some children, however, is often hard to come by. The fall of humankind, the entrance of sin into the world's system, and incredible ongoing family dysfunction throughout generations leaves many children living in less than idyllic family structures.

Two points, though, must be made here. First, while researching and writing on the problem of evil and suffering is beyond the focus of this particular volume, we can rest assured that God can and is undertaking amazing generational-reversing work even in ongoing, harmful, and damaging family environments. A thorough reading of the Bible, in fact, candidly reveals that God more often than not chooses to work through seemingly broken families in order to bring his special purposes to pass.

The Molding Influence

Parents are the molding influence in a child's life. Anne Ortlund illustrates this in her book *Children Are Wet Cement*:

"That child of yours is helpless in the hands of the people around him. He is pliable to their shaping; they set his mold. What will he become?

That's what Abraham Lincoln asked—who never paid more than minimum courtesy to the adults whom he passed on the street, but when he passed a child, he stepped out of the way and doffed his hat.

'These adults I know,' he said, 'but who knows what the children may become?'

These little ones, kicking in their cribs or racing around—they are tomorrow's world, our most precious possession, most powerful potential. . . .

But the awesome thing is that they receive their impressions of life from us—even their impression of what makes godliness. . . .

Well, they are God's wonderful gift to us. Certainly they make us what we would never be, if they weren't watching us and copying us!

They are the arrows from our bows, with their direction dependent on our guidance.

They are the receivers of our batons, when we begin to tire.

They are tomorrow's heroes and rescuers and achievers—or else tomorrow's thieves and saboteurs and loafers."[17]

Second, a child reared in a less than stellar environment in no way needs to be consigned, condemned, or relegated to a lifetime of failure. Through hope, hard work, and healing, God breaks the generational chain, or curse, of ongoing household dysfunction.

Friends

Though parents and family—grandparents, aunts, cousins, siblings—are the most influential element of any tween's life, there are also many influences outside the family unit—teachers, coaches, and religious and civic leaders. Friends by far, however, have the most impact on a child outside of a tween's own parents. Literature produced through family-studies research is replete with examples showing the importance of quality friendships. The fascinating point, though, is the relationship between secure parental attachment and qualitative friendships.

Studies show that children who receive responsive and sensitive parenting form an internalized picture of themselves as someone who is worthy of such care. In other words, the child reasons, *Mom and Dad take really good care of me. I must be pretty special.* Further, since children view themselves as worthy of receiving such parental care, they begin to extrapolate positively from those relationships outward, toward others, including peers.

In general, children who form secure attachments with their parents end up forming secure attachments with their friends. Children will choose friends based on their models of self. Their reasoning is, *Mom and Dad take really good care of me. I must be pretty special and should be treated that way by everyone.* One study proved that "aspects of the early parent-child relationship, including security of attachment, have been shown to predict competence in forming close friendships at ten years of age such that children who had positive early relationships with their parents were more likely to have a close friend at age ten."[18]

Another way to illustrate this truth is *like attracts like.* If I feel and believe I'm securely attached to my parents, I will generally seek out and attract others who view themselves in a similar manner.

This is great news for your tween. The fact that you're reading this book demonstrates your concern for the well being of your child, which also means that you're probably closely monitoring to whom your child is attaching. And more than likely the friends your child chooses will mirror a reflection of what your child sees in his own sense of self.

So how important are good friends? A recent study on the critical importance of friendship selection reports,

> Friends are thought to have a strong impact on adjustment during preadolescence. . . . During the early adolescent period, friendship is thought to serve numerous functions, including the provision of intimacy, security, and trust; instrumental aid; and norm teaching. Thus, forming and maintaining strong, qualitatively rich friendships becomes of central importance during late childhood and adolescence. Researchers have shown that with age, children become increasingly reliant on friends for support.[19]

Two ideas to note: (1) despite the fact that her friends are imperfect and will, on occasion, take your child away from you, they are critical to her; (2) the key ingredient to her developing positive friendships—the second most important relationship in her life—is still you. When your child is fuming about your "checking up" on her, remember that your concern is of paramount importance to her life.

Community Outside of the Family

In addition to noting the development of positive friendships, I cannot overemphasize the importance of tweens getting involved in their neighborhoods' or towns' ongoing community lives. Sociologists are now closely working with medical and behavioral scientists in an effort to turn around the deteriorating mental and behavioral health trends of children in the United States. These experts report that a lack of connectedness is behind many of the rising rates of depression, anxiety, conduct disorders, and thoughts of suicide.

These cutting-edge scholars advocate children becoming more connected in two ways. First, children should be involved in close connections with other people. Second, children should form deep connections to proper moral and spiritual teaching. In a recent special report titled "Hardwired to Connect," a team of family and society scholars encouraged families to support *authoritative communities*. They write,

> Authoritative communities are groups that live out the types of connectedness that our children increasingly lack. They are groups of people who are committed to one another over time and who model and pass on at least part of what it means to be a good person and live a good life. Renewing and building [these community groups] is the key to improving the lives of U.S. children and adolescents.[20]

I was raised in the heartland of the United States—Topeka, Kansas. For thirty years my father served as an elementary school principal. When he died of cancer at the age of fifty-eight, the school district named the school's structure the Edward R. Pettit Building. My family lived and breathed the midwestern values of community.

Thus, as the authors of the study quoted above might suggest, I was hardwired to connect. I was connected to a church we attended on Sundays. I was a member of Cub Scouts. I was involved in youth sports. My father was involved in local civic groups. People knew my name and were not afraid to question me about how I was doing. Is this true in your community and family? If not, why not? Can you work to help make your community a place where you and your child are connected and held accountable?

This connectedness is not only a key to accountability, it's also an important part of creating your child's sense of normalcy. As a youngster, about the time I began thinking our family was weird or out of touch, we would attend a pancake breakfast, a church program, or community-wide fund-raising event. At these events,

I would connect with other families of similar values and beliefs. I witnessed my parents engaging with others in the community. I saw friends and neighbors, and knew that I was a small part of a larger whole.

This is the wisdom and beauty of active participation in civic community, and healthy involvement with religious and extended

Beer, Alcohol, and Cigarettes for Tweens

The alcohol, tobacco, and beer industries quickly have recognized the value of the World Wide Web as a marketing tool for reaching tweens. The Internet is a large part of tween culture—with the added value that it's unregulated, with very little parental supervision. Sixty-two percent of beer and alcohol Web sites display "youth-oriented features." The marketers aim their vices at tweens by

- Linking smoking and drinking in ads with being "cool" and independent, and with risk-taking behavior (particularly physical risks).
- Placing ads in magazines with high adolescent readership.
- Having movie stars, especially those popular with young viewers, smoke and drink in films.
- Sponsoring rock concerts and sporting events.
- Placing advertising near schools—on billboards, in bus shelters, and in variety stores.
- Running ads during TV shows that have a high number of young viewers.
- Creating and extensively marketing "alcopops"—sweetened, lightly carbonated drinks that don't taste like alcohol but have alcoholic content (alcoholic fruit drinks and lemonades).[21]

family structures. Connecting with positive outside influences is a key ingredient in balanced parenting. You can't go it alone. You and your tween were created for community.

The Power of Christian Community

If you haven't done so already, I strongly advocate your honest exploration of Christianity with your tween. As I've mentioned, your preadolescent needs a healthy connection with others with whom he can explore moral and spiritual meaning.

The very best way to undertake this task is by studying the Bible with its absolute truths, and joining in a place of worship where Jesus the Christ is exalted. The Christian church is the ultimate authoritative community because God is the ultimate authority. He is the Father of all fatherhood, and he both reflects and models the type of loving role all parents should adopt. It was God who invented the concept of family in the first place. Family is his idea.

Joining in the activities of the church connects you with the person and work of God throughout history. In addition, you will be surrounding your tween with the kind of community that will aid in the developmental individuation/separation process your child needs to complete.

A four-year research study at the University of North Carolina found that teens in religiously active families (described as families who attend church, pray together, and read Scripture together) have stronger family ties than teens in families that are not religiously active. The research involved almost nine thousand students and demonstrated, "All three dimensions of family and parental religious involvement analyzed here (family religious activity, parental religious service attendance, and parental prayer) tend to be associated significantly with positive family relationship characteristics."[22]

Support in Community

When parents and children isolate themselves in gated suburban communities and cocoon for weeks on end, parenting can become a heavy burden that's difficult to enjoy. It's time for parents and children to come out for a breath of fresh air and engage in authentic community.

> Every day we read or hear of families cracking under the pressure to survive. Whether it's a father who takes his family hostage or a child who tortures small animals, these types of extremes are real and should be addressed early and quickly when warning signs emerge.

Again, God created the idea of family. The ideal support networks for parents are extended family members who may live in your area. But if no family members are present, the church or parish family should step in and help, or possibly friends from your neighborhood "tribe" or community.

Avoid getting to the point where you crack under the constant pressure of raising your children; know that help is available. There are those who want to come alongside and help lift the parenting load. There are those in your authoritative community who want the best for you and your family. You need only ask.

Does your tween feel connected to a larger group of people who have his best interests at heart? Are there people in your authoritative community who are upholding the same values and beliefs you hold and want to pass on to your son or daughter? Or is your child isolated and "at risk"? Is your tween involved in exploring deep friendships and spiritual meaning with other like-minded neighbors?

Seeking wisdom from above; casting off fantasies of perfect parenting; living in genuine community with like-minded parents; and practicing open, authentic communication can help us effectively prepare our tweens for adolescence.

Chapter Review

- Children ages eight to twelve enter into a normal developmental stage wherefrom they may emerge either confident in their own sense of self, or unsure of who they really are, floundering and flopping around like a fish out of water. Tweens by their very nature live and move be*tween* the warm, safe environment characterized by the nest or the "womb" of home and the unpredictable outside pull of the world. Tweens exist, then, relationally and emotionally between two polarities—"womb" and world.

- This state of existence—the pushing and pulling—indeed constitutes a crisis environment. These continual crises can create either danger or opportunity.

- You will need to be sensitive to the differences in the way females and males experience the separation process.

- Helping your tween balance activities and interests so that he becomes a "whole person" is your responsibility.

- Friends are the second most influential group to your tween—second only to you. Encouraging a healthy self-image in your tween is critical to her choosing positive, healthy friends.

- Community is essential to a developing tween. Not only do these groups provide a reality check for your tween, but they are also a place for you to seek out and receive help.

Chapter Discussion Questions

1. Why is it important that children learn to live with others in community? Why should parents get involved in church or civic activities? In which direction would your tween say your own family leans—toward isolation or involvement?

2. Children must first learn to exist relationally in their own families. Is your family close-knit? What does your family do to stay connected with one another? Do your tweens feel safe to be themselves within your family?

3. During the tween years, parents need to prepare children to emotionally break from their families of origin in order to

develop their own healthy sense of identity. In what ways are you preparing your tween for this inevitable break? Would you say your own tween is more emotionally desirous of remaining at home or leaving the home?

4. Friends are critical to a tween's development. Who are your tweens' friends? What are their families like? Do your tweens have friends whom you're concerned about? If so, what are some ways you can encourage your tweens to develop new friendships?

5. What steps have you witnessed your tween taking in "becoming his own person"? How have communities aided or hindered your tween in forming his own healthy sense of identity? What can you do to encourage your tween's participation in outside communities?

6. Why is it so difficult to practice balanced parenting? Give a recent example of finding a healthy balance in your parenting efforts. Which of your parenting practices have worked well and which ones have fizzled?

2

Preparing Your Tween to Leave the Nest

This Chapter's Big Idea

As they feel their tween beginning to emotionally *individuate* and *separate* from the family of origin, some parents employ too much control. Depending on the child, this can cause the tween to feel suffocated and either (a) stifles her normal self-exploration or (b) increases her desire to break free and rebel. On the other hand, some parents take an extremely disengaged hands-off approach and expect their tween to live life fully on her own in order to find out for herself how difficult the world really is.

Tweens and Baby Robins

A mature live oak tree stands in our front yard. Its branches sprawl over the yard and a full canopy of leaves shades the ground during the super hot Texas summers. Each spring, like clockwork, a robin flutters among the leaves and begins building her nest in one of the crooks of the branches. She gathers up necessary materials—frayed kite string, last week's grass clippings, scraps of discarded and weathered newspaper—as she designs and constructs her future maternity ward.

Nothing deters her from the appointed mission. I can run the lawnmower or fire up the weed trimmer, yet she returns to continue construction. Over time our children eventually take notice and we start keeping vigil on the nest building from the kitchen window. Then the magic morning dawns when several small, bright blue eggs appear.

I hoist our youngest children up to the edge and caution, "Don't touch!" They *ooh* and *ah* and can't believe their eyes as they announce to the neighbor kids, "We've got baby robins in our front yard!"

Just days later, chirping sounds emanate from the live oak and lure us out the front door to view the featherless baby birds, their necks craning and mouths gaping. For the next few mornings we watch the robin family squirm, feed, bob, and weave. Then the day arrives when we begin noticing frayed kite string and discarded scraps of newspaper dotting the grassy area under the branch. The kids wonder aloud, "Did someone mess with the nest?"

No . . . the mother robin herself dismantled the nest. Little children are often dismayed when told the sometimes harsh truths regarding nature and reality. *Why would Mom Robin destroy her own nest? Why can't the babies stay in their nest? It's too cold . . . windy . . .* (Fill in the blank) . . . *for the babies to be out on their own!*

But following heartfelt discussions, they agree it would be more tragic if the young robins *never left the nest*. They see the Creator of all living things at work in his infinite wisdom. The mother robin who carefully constructed her nest is the selfsame robin who slowly deconstructs her humble home.

The operative word here being *slowly*, or more accurately, timely. Because equally tragic to the robins' never leaving the nest would be if the robin abruptly kicked her young ones out of the nest before they were capable of spreading their wings and bracing for the fall.

While I'm certain robins parent with care, only humans have been given a conscience and a determination to glorify God with their decisions. People are not bound by the dictates of nature alone. They can call upon the Holy Spirit to empower their parenting choices. You have much to say about the process of leaving and uniting, which your child is experiencing. You don't have to be a passive participant in the dance of preadolescent development. You are an active partner in his self-discovery whenever you balance your responses to his decisions. Think of your differing responses as two opposing family behavioral spectrums.

The Leftwiches and the Rightsides

On the far left end of the spectrum is a mushy, marshy swamp family that scholars label *enmeshment*. It's a word that means just what it sounds like. This type of family is meshed together, much like the symbiosis stage when the child is still within the mother's womb. The whole family is viewed as always being one unit with no individual parts. Decisions cannot be made unless everyone in the family is involved. No one is free to express individual feelings or emotions because doing so may upset the equilibrium of the group.

In this type of family, no one is really responsible for his or her own actions because no one is really an individual. All family members are squished together into a tightly wound ball of attachment. Very little separation has taken place in this type of family because they all cling to each other in order to find an identity not as individuals but as a family.

In this unhealthy scenario, each family member is expected to live up to historically prescribed family norms and patterns, regardless of whether these are actually ever verbalized or not. We'll call this family the Leftwiches. And if the Leftwiches are anything at all, they are close as can be. They are as snug as a bug under a rug.

On the far right end of the spectrum is a highly separated, individuated family in which each individual member is totally responsible for his own behavior. An individual family member cannot place responsibility for his actions on another because there is no "other" in this particular system; there is only the self. There's plenty of room for self-exploration and discovery in this family because no one is relating to anyone else. Everyone is out doing his own thing. There is no emotional home base to check in with because individual family members have formed their separate identities outside of, not within, the family. We'll call this family the Rightsides. And if the Rightsides are anything, each is his own person.

While reading the descriptions of these two extremes, you may have found yourself assigning value to one or the other family or parts of both. You may have a preference as to whether you'd like to spend Thanksgiving at the Leftwiches, where everyone is expected to remain hovering around the table all day, or the Rightsides, where it's a quick bite to eat before everyone is out the door and off to their own agenda. Or you may now be expecting me to tell you about the family that fits right in the middle of the spectrum—the Goldilocks family, in which everything is *just right*. Sorry, there's no such thing as the perfect family.

The results of my research clearly indicate there is no perfect middle. There is no one-size-fits-all family system that I can prescribe for you to emulate. And in a real sense that's part of the beauty of family development. I've chosen to use the term *balanced parenting* because in order to form a healthy, well-adjusted family, you'll need to discover and explore your own preferred middle ground between individual closeness (cohesion) and personal space (separateness). At times you'll need to allow your tween to feel securely attached. At other times his need for safe exploration will need to be met.

Let's look at the research and an example of both extremes at work. In a survey of 870 adolescents, boys who reported high levels of emotional support from parents demonstrated significantly lower rates of early sexual behavior than those reporting low levels of support. These findings point to the importance of emotional support and may influence you to always keep your tween close by your side.

But in the very same survey, it was also reported that boys and girls who perceive their parents to be overcontrolling are more likely to initiate sex at younger ages than do those reporting less controlling parents.[1] So what's a parent to do—control or not control?

The best plan is a balanced approach to preparing tweens for adolescence. An outlook toward life that places responsibility on you *and* your child best sets your tween up for the inevitable approach of adolescence. By using balanced parenting you slowly hand off responsibility to your tween as she proves she is maturing and capable of mastering normal developmental tasks like finishing homework, handling money, completing chores, and regulating her own emotions.

> Antismoking campaigners are calling for tougher measures to protect children from tobacco after a study revealed they start to become addicted from the first puff.
> A five-year study of more than 1,200 children between the ages of seven and twelve found symptoms of nicotine dependence developed soon after tobacco was inhaled for the first time.[2]

In unhealthy families, responsibility is passed off to any number of variables. A son performs poorly in school and his father announces, "Don't look at me. I'm working two jobs already!" A daughter is cut from her school basketball team and her mother responds, "Don't worry about this, Jenny. I know several of the school board members. I'll get you on that team!"

Six Signs of a Strong Family

Based on the largest study ever recorded on strong families—14,000 families studied over twenty-five years—here are the six steps researchers recommend for building a strong family:

1. Commit to your family, commitment being the foundation on which the other five steps are built;
2. Express appreciation and affection;
3. Share positive communication;
4. Spend quality and quantity time together;
5. Nurture spiritual well-being;
6. Learn to cope with stress and crises.[3]

Christian Unity and Individuality

Balanced parenting promotes the idea that an individual is important as a part of a family—and that a family is important because it is comprised of individuals. The parts are as honorable as the whole because the whole is made up of honorable, individual parts. Both the parents and the tween are valued. This idea of oneness and community has been upheld within the Judeo-Christian tradition for thousands of years.

Christians believe that Jesus of Nazareth, the second person in a trinity of unity, took on humanity. Within the Trinity are three distinct persons that form one essence—three distinct persons within one family. Each person represents his own actions and the actions of the whole. This idea was reflected in Jesus' statement when he announced, "Truly, truly, I say to you, the Son can do nothing of Himself, unless it is something He sees the Father doing; for whatever the Father does, these things the Son also does in like manner" (John 5:19).

The theme of distinction within unity, or oneness without sameness, can also be seen when Jesus said, "For this reason the Father loves Me, because I lay down My life so that I may take it again. No one has taken it away from Me, but I lay it down on My own initiative" (John 10:17–18 NASBU). The notion is further highlighted in the intense Garden of Gethsemane struggle where Jesus requested, "My Father, if it is possible, let this cup pass from Me; yet not as I will, but as You will" (Matt. 26:39 NASBU). This inter-Trinitarian communication reveals that Jesus was both securely attached to the Father and securely individuated from him. Jesus' identity was secure in both who he was as Jesus, the second person in the Trinity, and as who he was as God, three persons in one essence.

When I was growing up, my parents did a wonderful job of finding balance. While my family was hardly the perfect Trinity, my parents emphasized that I was Paul—a unique individual with incredible gifts and talents. But they spent equal time emphasizing that I was also a Pettit, that there were five in our family and that we all lived under the same roof and were always to love and assist one another in the daily challenges of life. I enjoyed both roots *and* wings, free to be a unique individual and at the same time part of a pattern that made up a whole. I experienced both secure attachment and safe exploration.

Eugene Peterson, poet and Bible translator, communicates this idea in his paraphrase of Paul the apostle's words in his letter to the Romans:

> The only . . . way to understand ourselves is by what God is and by what he does for us, not by what we are and what we do for him. In this way we are like the various parts of a human body. Each part gets its meaning from the body as a whole, not the other way around. The body we're talking about is Christ's body of chosen people. Each of us finds our meaning and function as a part of his body. But as a chopped-off finger or cut-off toe we wouldn't amount to much, would we? So since we find ourselves fashioned into all these excellently formed and marvelously functioning parts in Christ's body, let's just go ahead and be what we were made to be, without enviously or pridefully comparing ourselves with each other, or trying to be something we aren't. (Rom. 12:3–6 MSG)

Balanced parenting requires that we study our children intensely and know them intimately, seeking wisdom to know when we are responsible for our children's actions and when they are responsible for their own. For example, like good church leaders should not allow church members to enviously or pridefully compare themselves to each other, we should not allow our children to do so with their brothers and sisters, or even their friends. In addition, we should discourage our children from being something they aren't. The passage above was written specifically for the church. But read it again. This time read it with your own family in mind.

Teaching Responsibility

As emphasized in the previous chapter, we were designed to live in community. And in community we are each responsible for our own behavior. Parents are responsible for the behavior of their children—up to a point. As children turn into tweens, and then into teens, a fuzzy developmental time period overlaps when children are kind of responsible for their own behavior and parents are still kind of responsible for their children's behaviors. Family scholars don't assign a numerical age to this phenomenon but announce that this can happen at age thirteen or sixteen or even eighteen, because each of God's creatures is unique and each child matures at a differing rate.

This change in responsibilities does not occur in one instant, but over a period of time. Over time, your child should begin to accept responsibility for his own behavior. If he doesn't, you may not have done your job of fully releasing your child—allowing him to grow up and make his own well-grounded decisions. If this is true, your child is in for a heaping portion of heartache.

Tweens Grow Up Quickly

The marketing industry is forcing tweens to grow up quickly. Industry research reveals that children eleven and older don't consider themselves children anymore. Further, the Toy Manufacturers of America have changed their target market from birth to fourteen, to birth to ten years of age. The Media Awareness Network says that by treating tweens as consumers, marketers have been successful in removing the gatekeepers (parents) from the picture—leaving tweens vulnerable to "potentially unhealthy messages about body image, sexuality, relationships, and violence."[4]

The opposite is also true. Placing too much responsibility on your tween when she is not mature enough to handle it causes disillusionment and discouragement. Pushing adult-like responsibilities on our young children is as unhealthy as allowing them to avoid age-appropriate behavior. Balanced parenting is the goal.

Avoiding responsibility plagues us all. I recently heard of an elementary school teacher lamenting to her colleagues about how one of her students said he would not be turning in his homework. The wily boy described to his teacher how his dog had pressed Ctrl+Alt+Delete! Avoiding promises and placing blame is a timeless and universal problem—one we all struggle with. This avoidance of responsibilities has not slowed, in fact, since the practice began with the first humans.

It Started in the Garden

God pointedly asked Adam why he had disobeyed. Adam replied it wasn't his idea to partake of the fruit, but the woman's, whom God had given to him. *It's actually* your *fault, God, not mine!* Next, Eve declared it wasn't her fault that she had disobeyed God but the serpent's, who tricked her. *It wasn't my fault, God. I was perplexed by a python!* This avoidance of responsibility has continued unabated since Eden.

I'll never forget the time I scolded one of my sons for throwing a football across our living room—something he knew was a no-no. He responded, "I wasn't really throwing it. I was just putting it up in the air." I should have replied, "I'm not really grounding you. I'm just putting you up in your room."

A Reasonable Amount of Responsibility

Letting our children avoid important tasks and babying our growing children is a disease we must inoculate against. We should not let our preadolescents skate by nor should we baby them for too long. *You didn't clean your room again, but don't worry about it. I'll do that later after I finish all of your laundry and tackle your math homework.* Children who grow up without any responsibility often become adults who continually expect others—the government, good luck, friends (who don't stick around long!), or even an incorrect notion of God—to meet all of their needs.

On the other hand, demanding too much responsibility from our children is also a plague to be avoided. We can't place supermature, adult-like responsibilities on our developing tweens. *As you know sweetie, we're behind in our monthly car payment again. Can we dip into your roller-skating money just one more time?*

Some children who grow up always playing the family role of "responsible adult" never quite seem to shake the feeling of, *If I don't do it, it's never going to get done!* We recognize these adults as ones who serve on every volunteer committee at church, school, and in their community. They feel guilty when they relax, and they view playing with their young children or participating in recreation with their tweens as wasting time. And why wouldn't they if they were never allowed to enjoy the constructive free time childhood affords.

Placing age-appropriate responsibilities before our children will help prepare them to face the approaching learning curve of the demanding teen and adult years. We do them no favor by shielding them, in the name of love, from the inevitable pains and difficulties that normal adolescence brings. As parents, you and I must even be willing to watch our children suffer—if that suffering helps them move toward more age-appropriate levels of responsibility. Nor do we pay them a favor, in the name of limits, by forcing them to parent alongside us or manage households that are not their own.

One of the main tasks of preparing our tweens for adolescence must involve teaching them to take responsibility for their own actions. They must understand that there are consequences to actions. Sequences of events are set off when choices are made. Young children do not possess the cognitive reasoning required to logically think through each of their decisions. They play Superman and jump from backyard balconies. They try to put on their own eye

shadow. *Wow, who got into mommy's makeup?* They ride skateboards
and scooters down hills that are too steep.

Too Much, Too Little, or Just Right?

In any given playground, you'll find pink-faced children flying
high on the swings, zooming down the slide, and bouncing up and
down on the seesaw. While there are certainly rules for the swing
and slide (you have to *let go* at the top of the slide in order to slide
down), the seesaw seems to require the most finely tuned execution.
First and foremost, unless a child likes to simply sit on a sloping
board, there must be two people to operate a seesaw. Second, if one
child is significantly heavier than the other, the lighter child is des-
tined to never touch the ground. It takes two balancing each other
for the seesaw to rock up and down.

The principle is the same for parenting a tween. It takes a steady
balance between parent and child. There needs to be give and
take—it takes both individuals working in tandem to send the
tween out successfully. So what do you do if you're struggling with
either not getting on the seesaw (undercontrolling) or putting too
much weight on one side of the seesaw (overcontrolling)? How do
you know if you're doing it right?

A recent best-selling business book, Stephen R. Covey's *The 7
Habits of Highly Effective People*, urged readers to keep in mind at the
outset of undertaking a new task the *end result* of that task. Let's do
that. For a moment, as an experiment, rather than thinking about
the process of parenting or the skill required, let's consider the end
result. Where are you headed with your parenting? What are you
attempting to accomplish? What will your parenting look like when
you're finished?

A difficulty arises in parenting tweens. While you were parenting
your newborn, everything seemed new and fresh. There were loads
of books, television shows, and advice columns on how to handle
an infant. Our infants were so young and impressionable at times
that it felt like parenting well involved reading from a checklist we
marked off. But as our children move into the tween stage, we often

become discouraged. While there are still resources to consult, the results don't seem to arrive as quickly as before. During the infant and toddler stage we were most concerned with behaviors. Now we are tackling thought patterns and emotions. As our children develop, our parenting patterns mature and develop as well. Over time, the *vision* of why we are attempting to parent well can, and often does, grow fuzzy.

As healthy parents, we raise our children in order to release them. While you may be neck deep in tween issues today, the fact is you are raising children who will one day soon grow up and move out. We spend considerable energy in our hopes that they will one day leave us and become adults, not children.

As you've probably learned by now, one of the most difficult parts of parenting involves knowing when to allow children to make their own decisions and when we as parents need to step in and assist. You can't always know on your own. It takes relying on your community of friends and on supernatural wisdom to parent well.

Spirit-filled Parenting

One of my current mentors, Dr. Howard Hendricks, often reminds me that parenting isn't difficult . . . it's impossible. That's why we desperately need the limitless power of the Holy Spirit to lead and guide us as we tutor our tweens. We find Spirit-led family advice from the apostle Paul in his letter to the Ephesians, giving instructions to both children ("Obey your parents"[6:1]) and dads ("Don't exasperate your children"[6:4 MSG]) But both of these commands are predicated by the admonition to "be filled [present tense, i.e., 'be being filled'] with the Spirit" (Eph. 5:18).

While Howard and Jeanne Hendricks were raising four children, they began using a rule of thumb for parental decision making. The child should continue in performing any task that the child had successfully proven he could perform on his own (task mastery). If one of their boys had successfully mastered the art of shoe tying, he was not allowed to approach Mom or Dad and whine, "Mom, will you tie my shoes again?" You get the picture.

How sad to see children who are developmentally delayed. All children face developmental challenges throughout their early years. How much valuable time and money has been spent on mastering toilet training? How many expensive video cameras have captured first steps? How satisfying it is to watch your child write her name for the first time! And yet some children fail to adequately progress within standard developmental norms and stages.

Separation and Individuation

As mentioned earlier, one of the normal developmental stages of preadolescence is what family researchers call separation/individuation. It's called separation because slowly your child will began to explore the world around her and slowly separate from you.

Just like when she was an infant, your daughter is beginning to realize she can make her own choices in life. She's beginning to question some of your decisions and judgments. She will separate from you emotionally so that she can become a person who is distinct or different from you. Again, at the tween stage, it's not so much a physical separation as an emotional or psychological one.

Your child will also individuate. That is, he will become his own *type* of person. Can you see the subtle difference between separation and individuation? He will separate from you (he is not a part of you; he will one day move away from you) and he will individuate himself (he will become different from you and everyone else, distinct, his own person).

> It is the nature of the human being that he finds fulfillment only in a broadened existence, and that for him life confined to the limits of one's individuality in segregation from others is worthless.[5]

As we practice balanced parenting with our preteens, we help them successfully navigate through these two processes of preadolescence. Research shows that those children who feel safe and secure with their parents (attached) are best able to expand and explore the horizons of who they are as a person. In other words, my children must feel safe and secure as a part of the Pettit family before they can investigate and explore who they are as individual Pettits.

Recently, as I was helping one of my sons with his science homework, I realized that helping raise an emerging tween is much like watching a beautiful butterfly develop. As you probably know, monarchs go through a process called metamorphosis. The starting point for complete metamorphosis begins with an egg. The larva then goes into the pupa stage, or resting period. The pupa builds a chrysalis and becomes encased in it. Finally, a monarch butterfly emerges from the chrysalis.

In this ancient cycle of development, one can see a picture of the human life span. In both the human and the monarch, a type of metamorphosis occurs. The baby is first encased in the mother's womb. The child is then encased in the chrysalis of the family. We could call this the resting period. The child is not ready to spread her wings and fly as an adult, but is preparing to do so. So much of what occurs in the pupa or resting stage, while she is encased in her family, is not seen by the outside world. And it is in this stage, the tween years, where you as a parent hold incredible influence.

While he was an infant and then a toddler you helped your child perform the majority of his tasks. You bathed, fed, clothed, and cradled him. Now that he is a tween you are required to do less and less for him. This is only natural. Your tween will soon be driving, working part-time jobs, and dating; so whether you fully realize it or not, each day you are heavily involved in the process of training your child to leave you. And when he leaves, he will take with him the life lessons he learned from you during the critical training time he spent under your roof.

During a family vacation, I was hiking in the Sangre De Cristo mountain range of southern Colorado. One of our guides, Larry, brought his six-year-old son, Elijah. At first, I thought Elijah wasn't going to complete the hike. Then, after a couple of difficult uphill miles, I thought I wasn't going to complete the hike. But little Elijah was just in front of me. And Elijah's father, Larry, was just in front of him.

Over time I noticed how Elijah just kept on, following in his father's footsteps. Actually, Larry was the only one who knew where we were headed. But that didn't stop little Elijah. He trusted his dad. And the interesting point I observed was that Larry trusted Elijah as well. Larry never doubted or babied Elijah. He just kept urging him on and led the way. What a wonderful example for parenting tweens. When we lead the way with love, encouragement, and trust, our tweens will desire to follow while learning to walk their own walk.

Learning to Let Go

How do we learn to emotionally let go of our tween and allow her to develop into her own person? What parenting skills should we adopt as our children move from toddlerhood to tweendom? In an earlier era, and in some cultures today, it is not uncommon for young teens to marry. The marriage ceremony normally involves—somewhere during the service—the father of the bride giving his daughter away to the prospective groom. There are usually tears shed in a healthy way by loving family members. This is a symbolic picture of one family releasing their daughter *into* the family of another.

No doubt you've heard a minister declare, "Who gives this woman to be married to this man?" And from the clutching, grasping father standing at his daughter's side, you've detected the faint, "Her mother and I." (The one line most dads have in the elaborate wedding they're footing the bill for.) Make no mistake. It is a real giving.

Whether the newlywed is a young man or a young woman, an honest leaving is involved. The words of Genesis 2:24 remind us, "For this cause a man shall leave his father and his mother, and shall cleave to his wife; and they shall become one flesh." The one flesh union is designed for a man and a woman in marriage; it is not a design for parents and their children. Since we are so close to our children emotionally, however, there is pain involved in watching them grow, mature, and leave us—even though the process is normal and healthy.

The amount of residual pain involved in the leaving is determined not on the day of the wedding, but now—as you are raising your tween. Yes, your little baby boy is going to grow up and leave the nest. Are you ready? Are you preparing for that transition now in both small and large ways? Will you allow your child to successfully leave or will you be the type that holds on and cleaves? The activities and parenting skills you employ while your child is young will go miles toward determining what the break from his family will one day look like.

A group of family researchers conducted a survey of successful young fathers, and three themes emerged from the data. First, these involved dads displayed *positive emotionality*, which was characterized as positive expressions of emotions about their children: *I'm proud of you*; *I love you*; *I'm glad you're my daughter*.

Second, these young fathers demonstrated what the researchers labeled *engagement*. They were not only emotionally involved, they also showed concrete expressions of interaction with their children. These engagements included attending events/activities together, playing together, and caretaking actions such as dressing and feeding.

The third theme was called *accessibility*, which measured how available—both physically and emotionally—the dads were to their children. For example, a daughter may yearn for her father to verbally describe the love he feels for his wife, and yet the dad says he can't. Or, a son may long for his dad to talk about his experiences in the Vietnam Conflict, but the dad says he prefers not to talk about it. These are examples of areas where a dad may not be accessible. Resolving these accessibilities issues would mean requiring a father to put into words the emotions he feels for his wife, or a dad writing down and recording his memories from Vietnam. The family scholars found resolving accessibility issues was very complex and would require fathers to develop more emotional maturity and parenting skills.[6]

One of the best ways for dads to grow in their emotional maturity is to get involved with a small group of like-minded dads. It's important for men to talk about the issues they're facing and hear that other dads are struggling with similar fathering concerns.

Many moms seem naturally to involve themselves in such groups. It is not uncommon for moms to discuss their current struggles regarding parent/child issues. Dads, on the other hand, do not normally discuss their fathering efforts without being asked or being involved in a class or discussion group.

Meaningful Discussions

If you're like most parents, your days fall somewhere between a continuum of *I'm so frustrated with my tween this afternoon, someone can come and collect him right now, thank you!* to *I can't believe how mature my tween is becoming. This preadolescence stage is no big deal after all.* During your parenting journey of learning to let go, you will experience days (weeks?) that involve wishing your tween would hurry up and grow up and move out, to days (moments?) where you dream about freezing time and wishing your tween could forever remain fixed in this innocent age. Experiencing both extremes of these emotions is entirely normal. Above all, though, remember that we raise 'em to release 'em. Our tweens are our God-given stewardship for only a few years. They are our gift and our responsibility.

We are often afraid to let go of our children and allow them to begin exploring the world outside of the family on their own. And yet how sad it is when we see tweens who are not allowed to do so in a healthy manner. For the sake of our children, we must learn to reject fear and practice trust.

Admittedly, it is difficult to watch our tweens prepare for the inevitable transition to adolescence. Dr. James Dobson describes the process succinctly:

It is common knowledge that a twelve- or thirteen-year-old child suddenly awakens to a brand-new world around him, as though his eyes were opening for the first time. That world is populated by age mates who scare him out of his wits. His greatest anxiety, far exceeding the fear of death, is the possibility of rejection or humiliation in the eyes of his peers.[7]

When your child was an infant and then a toddler, she felt safe and secure in your presence and in your home. But now, as she approaches the tween and teen years, she is facing issues of self-identity and questioning many of the assumptions she has always taken for granted. These questions include issues of beliefs, core values, habits, and worldview. If you are not available to talk with your tweens about the issues they are facing, who will?

Part of learning to emotionally let go of your tween and allowing him to develop into his own person requires that you talk with him about how he's doing and what he's dealing with. That *sounds* easy. But you and I both know that talking with tweenage children can be anything but simple. The good news is that there are parenting skills you can learn to make the going a bit easier.

One specific skill is to set aside times where you intentionally discuss with your tween what she's thinking and feeling. At first this may be awkward but your goal is to cover the ground your child is concerned about. Silence and distancing are danger signs during the tween period, so discuss even the hard topics. Talk about how your child's body is changing physically. Discuss her hormonal changes. Ask about the ideas and philosophies of her current friends. Listen to the music your tween is listening to. Practice being intentional with your tween as opposed to waiting for a bad report card from school or a knock on your door from the local police.

Another specific skill we can practice is spending quality time on our tween's turf. If you're like me, you probably expect your tween to enjoy the activities and lifestyle choices that you enjoy. But why not engage in your tween's favorite activities? Ask your tween to take you to the mall and point out the latest trends and fashions. Allow your tween to show you some tween-related Web sites where cool graphics and new lingo are used. Set up an appointment with your tween's school counselor or youth pastor. Immerse yourself in what an average day must be like for your tween. Take a day and look at life, and your home, through your tween's eyes. You may be surprised at what you see!

Cell Phones for Seven-year-olds

The Firefly Mobile is the first cell phone created especially for tweens. On the Firefly there are no numbers to dial. Instead, there are five buttons to push: a silhouette of a woman with a button labeled "Mom"; a silhouette of a man labeled "Dad"; a button featuring a picture of a phone book; a green "Start Call" button; and a red "End Call" button. As a safety feature, the phone blocks the tween from calling any numbers that haven't been entered by Mom or Dad, and no calls can be received that haven't first been stored in the phone.[8]

Preparing for Release

During the separation/individuation process the question will quickly become, *How much control do I take?* The next two chapters explore some common parenting tendencies. Be sure to read through both chapters as you may be surprised by what you'll discover about yourself or your spouse. In the meantime, you'll want to establish a group of people you can check in with to get a feel for your efforts during this stage.

The first person you can ask is God. Spend serious time in prayer, asking God to give you the wisdom to parent well. Pour out your heart before him and ask him to reveal weaknesses or breakdowns in your parenting efforts. Get brutally honest in his presence and ask him to show you how you can connect with your tween at the soul level.

The second person you can ask is your spouse. God normally guides opposite personality types to combine in marriage. One partner is more cautious. One partner is generally more relaxed. One is a spender, the other is a saver. You've heard that before. It will help your perception on this issue to go ahead and ask your spouse, *Do you think I'm too strict with the kids?* Or *Do you think I spend enough time with our son?* Your spouse will give it to you straight.

The third person you can ask is your tween. This is difficult. If you've never done so it may even feel awkward. But no one will give you instant, accurate feedback like your tween. After you wade through the preliminaries, like your daughter wanting an increase in her allowance and a later curfew, ask the serious questions about whether or not your tween feels comfortable enough to approach you with *anything* that is a current struggle. Yes, you need to be that close.

And fourth, ask a trusted friend. You can run a specific situation past a friend, asking if he believes you are being too strict or possibly not strict enough. If your friend senses you are genuinely looking for assurance he will give you his honest opinion, which you can weigh along with other opinions you're seeking. Remember, parenting is a process. It's not healthy to parent in isolation. Ask other parents for advice and encouragement.

Chapter Review

- Tweens move toward an emotional break from their families of origin. This is natural and normal; let them go. But balanced parents walk with them through it.

- Growing up involves separation (your tween is not a part of you; he will one day move away from you) and individuation (he will become different from you and everyone else, distinct, his own person).

- Children learn healthy responsibility by taking on small assignments first and then adding larger ones over time.

- Some tweens may feel as though they are being abruptly pushed into the world and quickly pulled back toward home at the same moment. The wise robin makes her nest a little more uncomfortable over time.

Chapter Discussion Questions

1. Where is your family on the spectrum between the Leftwiches and the Rightsides? Is your family functioning well where it is? If it is necessary, what can you do as a parent to shift your family?

2. Why is it important for parents to teach their tweens responsibility? What are a few things you can let your tween take on to help teach her responsibility?

3. Are there responsibilities that your tween has now that are too big for him? Is he given too much responsibility in regard to the younger children in the family? Does he act like a friend, listening to all of your complaints, concerns, and frustrations? What can you do now to help remove some of this burden?

4. An eight-year-old is begging her mom to take her to the skating rink. Yet her room is a mess, she's performing poorly in school, and she's already spent her weekly allowance. What advice would you give? Would taking the girl to the skating rink be a help or a hindrance to her development? Why or why not?

5. How is your tween beginning the processes of individuation and separation? How have you handled these situations?

3

When You
Overcontrol Your Tween

This Chapter's Big Idea

Parenting is a balancing act. Some parents end up putting an unfortunate amount of pressure on their tweens. This chapter addresses not only what overcontrolling looks like but also how to overcome it.

When I was in college, I served as an equipment manager for our school's football team. One of my tasks was to stand on the sidelines during the game and constantly maneuver the headphone cords of the special-teams coach. Since I was a rookie manager, my buddies, all older, more experienced managers, took delight in watching me try to keep up with this particular coach.

Here's how the job worked. As long as the coach was simply standing on the sidelines, watching the development of the game, life was good. But when the coach sprang into action, running up and down the sidelines, I was forced to keep up with his every step. As he ran between (and sometimes through!) three-hundred-pound linemen, I had to let out the length of the extension cord attached to his headphones. When he came back to his favorite spot, I had to reel in the cord so smoothly that he never even noticed. Oh how I wish he would never have noticed!

It turned out I was especially gifted at getting my coach's cords wrapped around almost every player's and coach's legs on the sideline. My coach would scream, "It's fourth down, we've gotta punt . . . we've gotta punt!" and he would sprint down the sidelines in hot pursuit of his punter. As I raced after him, the cord would tangle around legs and benches, and the headphones would inevitably jerk violently off of his head and thud to the ground. I never really acquired the knack for keeping up with my hyperactive coach. I've since seen him on television, though, coaching a professional team in the Super Bowl, and I told my kids he probably ended up doing so well in coaching because of my expertise with his headphones.

The not-so-subtle point of the story is this: in balanced parenting you are closely monitoring your tween, letting out and reeling in his freedoms, responsibilities, and challenges. The image I want you to retain is of me standing next to my coach during my very best moments, letting out just enough headphone cord for him to move about freely, and not reeling him in so tightly that we were wrapped side by side. (That did happen once.)

Each stage of a child's life blossoms with new activities, insights, and possibilities. The emotional, physical, mental, and spiritual aspects of their lives constitute a garden of possibilities.[1]

Why Releasing Your Child Is Necessary

It is critical that you practice slowly releasing your child so that she learns to live life on her own. You won't be there, physically present at her side, after she leaves your home, so your tween must learn to become her own person. Obviously, much of our lives as adults are lived alone, and we need to learn to make our own unique decisions and determinations about how we choose to live our own lives. We also need to learn how to live in harmony with others, balancing appropriate amounts of give and take. The graph below demonstrates the polarities of individuality and togetherness that constitute our optimal existence as humans.

One way to visualize this balanced involvement is to plot it on a line. On the far left side are characteristics that describe the "self" as an individual and that we each need to possess in becoming our own persons. On the far right side are characteristics that define the "self" as related to others and the legitimate needs we feel and experience as we yearn for connectedness and learn to relate to others.

Both sides of the chart contain God-given needs that are legitimate and real. Some children may lean toward one extreme and some toward the other. You may have two very different children in your home—one on each end of the graph. Both an overcontrolling and an undercontrolling parenting style can inhibit your tween's journey toward self-discovery. The star in the middle shows an equal regard for both needs and constitutes an idealized target or balanced-parenting approach.

Individuality	Togetherness
Autonomy	Groupthink
Self as individual	Self as part of group
Isolation	Involvement
Independence	Dependence
Differentiation	Enmeshment
Separateness	Connectedness
"I"	"We"

While I was overseeing my assigned football coach's headset, I experienced real fear. I was afraid that if I let out too much electric cord it would allow too much slack and my coach might get tripped up on his headset cord. It was a real, not an imagined, fear.

Why do some parents not let out any cord, and overcontrol their tweens? One of the main culprits is plain old-fashioned fear. Some parents are fearful of even envisioning their tween separating from or leaving their family of origin and striking out for life on their own. Therefore, they tighten their parental controls.

In my research on family systems, I've discovered three areas in which some parents are fearful. These are not always imagined fears—they are real, legitimate concerns and should be honestly addressed.

Poor Parenting Skills

Some moms and dads continually question their parenting efforts and are afraid, however vague the feeling may be, that something they're doing may be damaging their children. They second- and third-guess themselves to death. They are forever "checking in" and comparing themselves with other parents to see what sort of discipline systems or guidelines other parents are using.

Since they lack faith in their own efforts, they overcontrol in an attempt to make up for some secret parenting-knowledge skill they think they may not possess. In their minds there exists a vague *somewhere* where other parents are doing a good job. Many frightened parents are convinced that they are somehow messing up. So they enforce strict codes or rules to cover up their doubts and feelings of inadequacy.

Untrustworthy Tween

Another reason some parents cover their fear with endless rules and regulations is because they don't trust their tween. While other preadolescents can be trusted, these parents are convinced that their own tweens are going to get in trouble at every turn. So they put their tween on an ever-shorter leash, never allowing him to explore his world. They doubt their child can handle any real responsibility and continually quiz him on his behavior. These parents are often on the lookout for trouble or are overly suspicious of any strange behavior.

Is God Not Enough?

The third reason some parents overcontrol due to fear is because they lack faith in God. Some parents are not aware or have a hard time comprehending that God loves their children and has their best interests at heart. Some parents reason that, since they've been unable to fully trust God in the past, there's certainly no reason why they should begin now—especially with their children! This faulty logic would have parents believe that they are more loving, powerful, and all-knowing than God. Some parents incorrectly believe they can stop future events from happening by placing tight constraints on their children's activities.

Where the Fear Comes From

I love what Jesus taught his disciples one day on the side of a mountain when he announced, "Do not be anxious then, saying, 'What shall we eat?' or 'What shall we drink?' or 'With what shall we clothe ourselves?'" (Matt. 6:31). We could easily add to this fear-based list the question we often ask, *What's going to happen to my tween?*

Jesus continued, "For all these things the Gentiles eagerly seek; for your heavenly Father knows that you need all these things. But seek first His kingdom and His righteousness; and all these things shall be added to you. Therefore do not be anxious for tomorrow; for tomorrow will care for itself. Each day has enough trouble of its own" (Matt. 6:32–34).

Wow, what an antidote to worry! We should not waste our days constantly worrying about or for our tweens. And yet oftentimes we worry and doubt God's protection and provision. Why is that? Let's dig deeper.

Past Harmful Experiences

Many of you reading these words have suffered through very difficult circumstances. You may even be thinking, *Trusting God with my tween is fine for some parents, but you don't know what I've been through!* You may have experienced pain-filled days as a child or wrestled with trying times. What parent would want a similar experience for her child? It may be difficult for you to slowly let go of your tween and allow her to make a few important decisions on her own. You've been there and things didn't go smoothly. You're only trying to use your wisdom to protect your child.

Or perhaps an older child of yours has been injured or harmed and you're overcompensating for that loss. You tell yourself, *I will keep* this *child close and I will not allow the pain to return again.*

Television Viewing Harms Educational Pursuits

The more time children spend watching television the poorer they perform academically, according to three recent studies. The American Academy of Pediatrics has urged parents to limit children's television viewing to no more than one to two hours per day—and to try to keep younger children away from TV altogether. In these recent studies, children who regularly watched television before the age of three ended up with lower test scores later on, and children and adolescents who watched more television were less likely to go on to finish high school or earn a college degree. The analysis of 1,800 children over a decade showed television watching was linked to poorer cognitive development among children younger than three and between the ages of six and seven.[2]

Too Much Media

It may not even be your own experiences that terrify you. It seems we hear horror stories concerning children in the news media on a daily or even hourly basis. It's obvious that our culture has changed since the days when children were free to roam neighborhoods unchecked. Our parents or grandparents were probably unfamiliar with child identification kits or the idea of planting homing devices in our children in an effort to locate them if they are ever lost, kidnapped, or abducted.

It's likely, however, that far too many parents are ingesting way too much media as they raise their tweens. Reading, listening to, or viewing a constant barrage of scary stories, night after night, will only serve to bring fear and doubt into your parenting efforts.

News outlets are constantly scouring the country looking for sensational, mostly negative stories to pass along. Thus, being too focused on media can lead to a parent's living in unnatural fear. Practicing balanced, faith-filled parenting requires we reject fear and trust in God, our own life experiences, and even our tweens.

The Balancing Act: Rejecting Fear and Practicing Trust

Most of us are familiar with the "trust fall." One person stands up on a chair or stool with his back facing the rest of the group. The group stands with hands intertwined, ready and waiting to catch the falling individual. No one is hurt *if* the individual trusts the rest of the group to catch him.

You, too, need to trust the foundations you've laid for your child. How would the individual standing on the chair learn to trust if her mother constantly stood by, holding on to her arm? Allowing your child to take the plunge into adolescence is a scary prospect. How do you know she won't land on the ground and end up with a concussion or broken arm?

Here are three proven practices for overcoming fear and the tendency to overcontrol our tweens in our parenting efforts.

Trust in God

The first step involves an absolute trust in our loving God. We must lay open our hands and give our tweens to God. We need to remember that we are only stewards in the parenting process. Our children are not really ours, they are God's. You may have offered your infant up to God during some type of infant or baby dedication ceremony. But have you done that lately now that your child is a tween? You might pray, *God this is your child. Thank you for allowing me the privilege of raising her until it is time to release her into the world. This day I give her to you once again as I serve as her shepherd. Thank you for this stewardship.*

After we have given our tweens to God, we must sincerely trust that God is at work. Once we symbolically take our hands off of our children and entrust them into God's care, we must trust in God to bless our parenting efforts. A beautiful picture of trusting in God can be seen in the book of Genesis when God asked Abraham to sacrifice his son Isaac as a burnt offering. Can you imagine? Would you or I have had enough faith in God to carry out such a task? Would you have been able to trust God over such a difficult assignment?

As Abraham lifted his glistening knife overhead in order to plunge it into his young, bound son, a ram appeared in a nearby thicket and the angel of the Lord said, "Do not stretch out your hand against the lad, and do nothing to him; for now I know that you fear God, since you have not *withheld* your son, your only son, from Me" (Gen. 22:12, emphasis added).

The comparison is stark: either we are trusting in God and have given our tweens over to the Lord, or we are *withholding* from the Lord in our attempt to control our children. God sees our parenting as an act of worship and giving. Trusting the Lord is our only real alternative as we parent our tweens. Just as Abraham laid down his son Isaac, have you genuinely given your son or daughter to the Lord? How often do you remind yourself that your parenting efforts are a stewardship?

Trust in Your Own Parenting Efforts

A second way we can overcome the tendency to overcontrol our tweens is by learning to trust our own parenting efforts. As previously discussed, some of us are so fearful of incorrectly parenting our tweens that we ignore our own parental instincts. When our children were younger, we instinctively knew they were not to run into the street or play with matches. These parental prohibitions were easy to enforce because we were convinced of their wisdom.

But as our children become tweens, we begin to doubt ourselves and our parental decisions. We begin to second-guess ourselves: *Since all of the other kids are going to the heavy-metal rock concert and then spending the night at the hotel, maybe we should just let Ty go?*

In addition to your trusting God, I urge you to trust your own parenting skills. Deep inside you know what's right for your tween. God has given you the necessary skills and resources to parent your tween well. Don't be afraid to ask for help—you'd be surprised at the wisdom of parents, neighbors, and friends. And don't be afraid to rely on your inner voice of conviction when you know you're making the right decision. Remember *you* are the parent and you have a life of experience on your resume. More than likely you've been through many of the situations and challenges your tween is preparing to undergo. And, while you shouldn't overact based on your negative experiences, you do have a knowledge base to draw from as you point your child in the right direction before letting go.

Dr. Ross Campbell described the end result of parenting when he wrote, "The ultimate goal in rearing children is to prepare them for responsible and happy and successful adult lives. This means you anticipate for your children, since they cannot do this for themselves. . . . They need for you to lead and anticipate and train, not merely react to their behavior."[3]

Five Characteristics of a Functional Family

We've all heard of the dysfunctional family. Yet what comprises a functional family? Relationship expert Dr. Gary Chapman lists five characteristics of healthy families:
1. An attitude of service
2. Intimacy between husband and wife
3. Parents who teach and train
4. Husbands who are loving leaders
5. Children who obey and honor parents[4]

Trust in Your Tween

Many parents who overcontrol simply need to trust their tweens. Learning to let go of a too-controlling parenting style involves learning to give your tween trust and responsibility. With added trust comes added responsibility. Ask yourself, *Do I really trust my tween?* If you are unable to answer in the affirmative, more than likely your child is picking up on that. It isn't easy to change those deep-seated feelings. So start with consciously making an effort to *act* like you trust your tween. Give her the room to pleasantly surprise you.

Recently, I started changing the way I talk to my children. In the past, as I dropped them off at their friends' houses for birthday parties or sleepovers, I would begin a litany of cautions as we approached the house: "Don't break anything, and whatever you do don't fight with anyone and I hope you remember your manners. . . ." I'd ramble on, continually adding to this speech anything I thought could possibly go wrong.

Lately, however, I've taken to using the opposite approach. In an effort to emphasize the positive and demonstrate my trust in my tweens, I'll remind them, "I'm sure you're going to have fun, so make sure you act like a Pettit." Why burden them with an endless list of potential problems when I can sum up how I really feel about them by saying, "I trust you to do the right things tonight. Now go make me proud!"

This is how God the Father spoke about his Son when he announced to a listening crowd, "This is My beloved Son, in whom I am well-pleased" (Matt. 3:17).

One of the best ways to show respect to your tween is by giving him small jobs or responsibilities and then adding on to these as they are fulfilled. We need to walk with our tweens, of course, as they learn these tasks, and reward them for jobs well done. But performing everyday tasks for our kids, tasks that they could accomplish on their own, shows them we do not trust them.

Popular Bible teacher Charles Swindoll posed the proper question surrounding responsibility in the life of tweens:

> If your growing youngster can't cut it at home in such things as cleaning up his room, making his bed, and earning part of his own way by the time of maturity, what on earth will he do when he faces a business career and marriage and the pressures of life?[5]

Forgiveness for the Past

As mentioned earlier, many parents have experienced harmful circumstances during their childhoods. These harmful experiences may have included instances of abuse or simple misunderstandings between them and their parents. The frustrating thing is that the effects of these memories may only surface during your parenting struggles—just when you most need a clear head. The good news is that there are many adults who suffered physical, sexual, and emotional abuse as children and yet became fine parents.

The keys to overcoming these profound struggles are seeking advice from a professional counselor and learning to forgive those who have inflicted harm. Suffering from past hurts and wounds often ends up sabotaging our best parenting efforts. If you don't feel the freedom to truly trust your tween, you may need to reevaluate whether you are harboring any anger or resentment from the past.

The efforts of overcontrolling parents to keep their children safe and secure may end up only hurting the children. The parents may reason, *I was hurt, but I am never going to let my child get hurt the way I was.* Forgiving the offender and then learning to trust in God for the welfare of your tween is the best way to raise healthy, well-adjusted kids. Never underestimate the power of parenting with forgiveness and balance.

It's sad to see a butterfly trapped in a cocoon. And it is equally discouraging for tweens if they are not allowed to learn by exploring, discovering, growing, and soaring.

> ### What Tweens Worry About
> - Difficult homework: 71 percent of girls, 68 percent of boys
> - Getting good grades: 59 percent of girls, 60 percent of boys
> - Their appearance: 54 percent of girls, 55 percent of boys
> - Making parents proud: 43 percent of both girls and boys[6]

News in Balance

A caution is in order here. Keep media messages in balance. Spending inordinate amounts of time watching television news or reading Internet crime reports can skew our perception of how safe or dangerous our neighborhoods are.

We need to be cautious, of course, and practice safe parenting habits with our children. But filling our minds with a constant stream of negative, sometimes sensational reports, can cause us to begin to live in fear. This fear can be unintentionally passed down to our tweens.

According to National Public Radio's Jeffrey Dvorkin, "Studies show that a disproportionate amount of ink and airtime devoted to crime tends to raise anxieties and exacerbate social tensions in communities." Dvorkin calls the culture of crime reporting an "interesting phenomenon" and cites Lawrence Friedman's *Crime and Punishment in America*:

> Crime reporting has risen by 700 percent in the United States since 1970, even as the nation's crime rate has declined by 4 percent during that same period. The country is actually safer than it used to be, but you might not be able to tell that from following the news in local papers or on local radio or television.[7]

A requirement of balanced parenting involves allowing our tweens to spread their wings and explore the outside world. Soon enough, our children will be burdened with the adult pressures of the marketplace. By learning to reject our fears and insecurities and by practicing trust in God, in our own parenting efforts, and even in our own tweens, we free ourselves to enjoy the parenting process for what it really is—an exciting journey of discovery.

Chapter Review

- The number one reason some parents overcontrol their tweens is fear.

- Parents tend to fear that their parenting skills aren't up to snuff, that their tweens aren't trustworthy, and that God isn't big enough. These fears generally come from past experiences and sensationalized media coverage.

- Media outlets portray an unusually large proportion of disastrous stories involving children. These percentages do not reflect the realities of most communities.

- The keys to rejecting fear involve trust—of God, yourself, and your tween—forgiveness, and balance.

Chapter Discussion Questions

1. Are there any serious fears in your life that need to be addressed? What are they? How will you go about tackling them?

2. How could ingesting a constant stream of sensational media stories cause you to overcontrol your tween?

3. An overly controlling mother acknowledges she was emotionally abused as a child. In what parenting areas would she likely struggle? What counsel or advice would you give? How would you help her learn to parent with trust?

4. It seems like overcontrolling should work. If we strictly limit the activities of our children to only those things we approve, won't they adopt our beliefs and mind-set? Yet why does over-controlling often backfire?

5. How can you check to see if you are parenting with love and limits? What do your neighbors and friends say about your parenting? Does your tween still have the same "bedtime" as five years ago? Why is that? Do you ever let your tween select the rented video? Why or why not? Are there areas in which you tend to overcontrol your tween? What can you do to overcome your fears in those areas?

6. You've probably heard the common phrase, "rules without relationship leads to rebellion." Why is that?

4

When You
Undercontrol Your Tween

This Chapter's Big Idea

While overcontrolling a tween is a recipe for disaster, so is under-controlling or emotionally abandoning a tween. This chapter looks at why a healthy balance is necessary and lays out ideas to help parents take appropriate control and set loving, meaningful limits.

When we hear the word *Columbine*, we instantly remember the images. The date was April 20, 1999; the location, Littleton, Colorado. Those of us who sat transfixed in front of television sets won't soon forget the horrifying pictures that blazed across our screens on that ugly day. Preteens and teens scrambled through broken windows and scurried out of sniper-covered doorways into the waiting arms of S.W.A.T. team units.

What strange forces would cause two teenagers—Dylan Klebold and Eric Harris—to plan and carry out a massacre at their own school, against their own classmates? Why would some children view these dysfunctional boys as heroes who "went down in a blaze of glory"? And what counteracting drives would cause two completely different teenagers—Rachel Scott and Cassie Bernal—to emerge from the same shootout as Christian martyrs? (Police investigative reports revealed that before firing, Harris looked into Bernal's eyes, pointed the rifle before squeezing the trigger, and mockingly asked, "So, you believe in God?")

It would be simplistic and wrong to attempt to ascribe reasonable explanations to why some teens experience a complete identity meltdown during adolescence. Other teens, from the very same school environment, were apparently secure enough in their identity and even served as Christian leaders on their campus. But research does show that both healthy and unhealthy adolescent trajectories can be positively or negatively shaped during the sensitive tween years.

As stated earlier, tweens begin to explore their own identities during the preadolescent developmental stages of individuation and separation. Throughout, this book has continually advocated a balanced approach to effecting our children's healthy breaking away from their families of origin.

After reading through the previous chapter, you may begin to think overcontrolling your tween is the worst possible harm you could bring to your child. When we overcontrol our children, we crush their spirit. Excessive rules and regulations hold them down, discourage their efforts to grow and to investigate the world around them, and clips their wings. The harmful effects of overcontrol can include your child wanting to run away from home, your child becoming depressed and contemplating suicide, or your child attempting to numb themselves or drown you out with alcohol or drugs. Yes, overcontrol is that serious. Equally troublesome, though, is the practice of exercising too little parental control.

Why Control Is Necessary

I'm fascinated by a concept the apostle Paul employs in his letter to the Ephesians. Paul first reminds children to obey their parents "in the Lord" in chapter 6, then he calls on fathers to not "exasperate" their kids (NIV). *Exasperate* means literally "to make angry." (A similar word is used in Colossians 3:21 in the New International Version, "Do not embitter your children, or they will become discouraged.")

The apostle gives us, in essence, a contrast: We either are bringing up our children "in the training and instruction of the Lord" (Eph. 6:4 NIV), or we are failing to bring them up—and by inference even tearing them down—by embittering them and making them angry. For many years I operated under the assumption that a child became bitter and angry only if his parent was always in his face. I thought a child became discouraged and exasperated by a parent who yelled or constantly "rode their child."

But I have since come to learn that children can become equally frustrated by absentee or underinvolved parents. It is the parents' responsibility to instill in their children an image of self-worth, but where there is no vision, the children cast off restraint. They reason, *I must not be worth my parents' time or attention.* That's why the term Paul uses for the type of care we are to take with our children is a word used for nursing. Paul says we are to act "tenderly" (1 Thess. 2:7) toward our tweens; we are to cherish our children (KJV).

No one else can bring them up. That's our job as parents. Tweens cannot bring themselves up. They need an older, wiser guide, someone who's traveled down the road a bit further then they have. We cannot force our children, we cannot jerk them up or mechanically crank them up; we must tenderly, lovingly bring them up. In addition, we cannot idly sit by and hope they grow up on their own. They need our active, balanced involvement.

On the next page is the graph used earlier, showing balanced involvement and the star plotted in the parenting "sweet spot." On the far left side are those characteristics that describe the self as an individual and the legitimate needs we experience in our journey of becoming our own persons. On the far right side are the characteristics that we need in defining the self as we learn to relate well to others.

> Identity is one of the pivotal developmental tasks of adolescence. A coherent sense of identity helps to organize and give meaning to one's experiences and to guide one's decisions and behaviors, whereas a fragmented, confused, or poorly structured sense of identity may render one especially susceptible to external events.[1]

Individuality	Togetherness
Autonomy	Groupthink
Self as individual	Self as part of group
Isolation	Involvement
Independence	Dependence
Differentiation	Enmeshment
Separateness	Connectedness
"I"	"We"

In the middle, we've placed the star to show our balanced-parenting target. Both sides of the graph include healthy characteristics that tweens need to develop. If, however, we parent exclusively on one side or the other, we miss the healthy balance that both sides bring.

In the middle we find harmony, shalom, balance, interdependence, the idea of being a separate yet connected self. We discover the ability to establish in our tweens the "I" *within* the "we." The goal of individuation is the tween's gradual, or age-appropriate, learning to take personal responsibility for her life. This requires a new way of thinking about the parent-child relationship.

The plotted star on the graph line is, however, only an idealized middle. You and you alone know what your tween needs. There is no simplistic, easy approach to your efforts at helping your tween meet these needs. Maybe your tween feels a greater need to learn his own story, to become a secure individual who is not swayed by the wrong crowd. On the other hand, maybe you sense your tween leans toward becoming a loner and needs to learn to enter into relationships and share emotionally with others. Since you are the parent, you are the closest and best equipped person for making these important determinations.

When I was growing up in Kansas, our back yard invariably contained a vegetable garden. I was always fascinated with the tomatoes. The vines quickly sprang up and almost overtook our backyard fence. Soon the green tomatoes would emerge and I knew the red, ripe tomatoes would shortly grace our kitchen table and make starring appearances in my mother's salads. But to get the large, juicy tomatoes onto our plates at just the right time, our timing had to be impeccable.

If we pulled them from the vine too soon they wouldn't be ripe but green, hard, and bitter. If we went on vacation or neglected the plants, they would languish in the garden and the tomatoes would become soft, mushy, and diseased, practically unusable. (My younger brother and I could still throw them at each other.)

So it is with parenting. Our timing needs to be accurate. We need to pay attention to those sensitive times when our tweens need our active involvement. We need to be cautious of those moments when they need feeding, pruning, nurturing. And we also need to be acutely aware of when we should back off and allow our tweens to grow, to solve problems without our help or make important decisions of their choosing. Bottom line—we need to allow our tweens to flourish with just the right amount of parental involvement.

Doing so takes much prayer and concentrated observation. The goal is to have more ripe tomatoes than rotten. One family researcher eloquently described the process advocated in this book as walking between tightropes.

> Adolescence is the start of the great process of differentiation. To learn who you are and who you want to become, a person must navigate between two thin tightropes, skipping between continuing and deepening ties with the family, while at the same time separating and distancing from them. Great interpersonal competence is required to pull this off successfully. Negotiating when and how to express closeness and intimacy, as well as when and how to express independence and autonomy, is a complicated art.[2]

As tweens practice separation and individuation, they are actually "trying on" new personalities and personas. They may actively discuss what they desire to become in the future. This discussion, though, will often change from one day to the next. This is because your tween is unsettled in her values. She may currently believe, for example, that the most important person in your community is the one who can perform an outrageously difficult skateboard trick.

Your tween's continual morphing is one of the reasons it's critical that you deeply, fully engage at a heartfelt level during these key discussion times. It may seem your child no longer needs your constant attention. In most circumstances, your child is now able to bathe, clothe, and feed himself. And as you see him undertaking these tasks, you may think your role is somehow now less important. Nothing could be further from the truth! You are needed now more than ever.

In my ongoing work with parents and children, I've found four reasons why some parents undercontrol their children.

Tweens on the Internet

Researchers are surprised by the speed at which children adapt the Internet to their own uses and interests. The Internet can become a way for tweens to experiment with different images and places as they seek out their own self-identity. Amanda Lenhart of the Pew Internet and American Life Project says, "A teen may be a biology and ballet student offline, but she becomes 'darkgirl79,' and goes to Goth blogs to experiment with that kind of personality, but not be seen that way by her ballet friends." Many tweens now have their instant messages forwarded to their cell phones for an "always on" connection. Tweens nowadays talk about meeting online, dating online, and even breaking up online.[3]

Some Parents Had Little or No Boundaries as a Child

As we set boundaries with our own children, we are at the same time teaching them to set personal boundaries in their own lives. Many parents had the unfortunate experience of being raised with loose boundaries and do not pass on healthy boundaries to their children.

My parents were raised in a quiet, rural setting. Safety issues were not the concern that they are today. Everyone left doors and windows unlocked or unchecked, including my home of origin. Today, however, most parents would never dream of going to sleep without locking doors and possibly double-checking the home security system.

You may have grown up freely exploring the town in which you were raised. At a very young age, you may have spent the entire day away from home, playing or discovering. You may have had very few boundaries placed upon your ability to ride your bicycle, talk to friends, or play with classmates. Since there were few boundaries placed upon you, you may not see a problem with giving your children limitless freedoms to roam and explore.

Yet cultural changes force us to look differently at our surroundings. As emphasized elsewhere in this book, yesterday's teens are today's tweens—your tween is being forced to make decisions and choices at a much younger age than you and your contemporaries were—and it is likely that your current neighborhood is not like the safe environment you enjoyed as a child.

In addition, many of today's parents didn't have boundaries set for them because their parents weren't around to enforce them. During the 1960s and 1970s, many full-time, stay-at-home moms entered the marketplace to begin careers, thus expanding the number of day-care babies and so-called "latchkey children." Just because a certain lack of boundaries was appropriate in the past doesn't mean it's appropriate now.

Some Parents Are Unaware of Current Dangers

Another factor that causes some parents to provide too-little control over their tweens is a certain naivety or lack of knowledge about today's issues. The overriding fact in current research is that children are feeling the pressure to grow up at a much quicker rate than previous generations.

Today's advertisers and marketers push sexuality upon children by offering adult clothing, music, and movie options to children. Girls are pressured to purchase makeup, push-up bras, and dieting products. Jane Buckingham, president of a consulting firm that forecasts youth trends, notes,

> The girls 8 to 12 years old are growing up so much faster . . . they're incredibly sophisticated, incredibly savvy, and incredibly brand-conscious. I think a 10-year-old is a lot more like a 14-year-old now than she used to be, and I think a 14-year-old is more like an 18-year-old than she used to be. I think it's a hard time to be a young girl . . . they may not be quite ready for the things being thrown at them.[4]

Some Parents Are Preoccupied with Their Own Lives

A third reason some parents undercontrol their children is simply because the parents are too busy. As our children arrive in the eight- to twelve-year-old age bracket, most parents are busy advancing their own careers, which can be good and healthy. How, after all, could a parent pay for food and invest for college without a well paying job?

An unfortunate condition in today's marketplace, though, is the not uncommon situation of employers' asking their workers to contribute ten or more hours per day on the job site. Simply put, many of us are so preoccupied with work, workplace issues, promotions, layoffs, and workplace conflicts that we fail to give our tweens the attention and nurturing they crave. When our tweens begin to believe that our work is more important than our families, they will look elsewhere for the affirmation and answers that the tween years demand.

> ## Planned Neighborhood Offers "Sex Offender-Free Zone"
> A planned subdivision in Lubbock, Texas, is offering a neighborhood with criminal background checks for homeowners and a guarantee of no convicted sex offenders. Experts predict if the idea catches on in Lubbock it will spread to other communities. Rula Maabra and her husband have children ages six and eight and says her family is weighing a move to the neighborhood because two registered sex offenders live within two blocks of their Lubbock home. "You can't protect your kids a hundred percent, but knowing that the street I'm living on and the ones nearby doesn't have one, makes me feel much better."[5]

Some Parents Had Overcontrolling Parents

Some overly lenient parents are overcompensating as a reaction to being brought up by extremely strict parents. Parents who fall into this category recognize the harm nooselike control can cause. So they figure the key is to be the opposite of their parents. Without recognizing it, these parents end up not providing the boundaries, rules, and relationship their tweens long for.

A Benevolent Authority

We've established this fact: a dangerously low level of parental involvement is not the best way to prepare your child for life. This is true despite the claims of social psychologists who tell us children are essentially good and need only encouragement along their journey toward adolescence. This advice sounds reasonable but doesn't square with Scripture.

Christian educator Dr. Kenneth Gangel admonishes,

> Parents need to understand not only the nature of their own children, but the true nature of all children born into the human race. Viewing children as essentially good leads to a permissive family government. For too long we have been led to believe that children left to their own devices and given ample love will develop in positive directions. The Bible teaches that children are neither good nor neutral at birth (Ps. 51:5; Eph. 2:3). They possess a sin nature that must be controlled and ultimately changed by the power of God. In understanding that, the wise parent exercises a benevolent authority given by God.[6]

A "benevolent authority" may sound like an oxymoron at first hearing. How does one exercise, at the same time, love and limits? Sure, it's a difficult task. That's why we are entirely dependent upon the Holy Spirit of God to give us unusual insight and wisdom as we raise our tweens. We need special insight not only into our developing tweens but also into ourselves. So how do we exercise love and limits at the same time?

One of the ways is to be on the lookout for a middle way. Say your twelve-year-old daughter comes to you and wants to go to a party a friend is throwing from seven in the evening until midnight. The overcontrolling parent may dismiss the notion outright. *Over my dead body are you going to a party with boys present, young lady!* At the other end of the spectrum is the absentee parent who is under-involved. *Oh sure, sweetie, just be quiet when you get in. I'll leave the garage door open 'cause I don't want you to wake me up.*

A balanced approach that provides healthy boundaries might be to discuss the evening first with your tween. By asking a few probing questions and making a few phone calls to other parents, your tween will quickly understand the importance you place upon such a request. Next, you could settle upon a halfway point in the request. A nuanced reply shows your tween that she is trusted, but also that you still know what's best. *Since we know the parents, we're going to let you attend. However, instead of midnight, we'll be by to pick you up at ten.*

Become Aware of Today's Dangers

Emerging cultural dangers is an area in which it's easy to get behind. It seems that new technology is announced every few weeks. Sin abounds in our lost and broken world. But we can't hide our children at home under lock and key in an effort at keeping them protected from the world. Sooner or later our children must travel alone to summer camps, go with their classes on field trips, or spend the night at friends' homes. And it is at those moments—when your child may be confronted with evil—that he will need the wisdom you have already instilled in him.

Is today's world that much different than the one you and I were raised in? Of course! Times change, cultural boundaries move, and society's standards relax. Today's glaring headlines demonstrate this drastic shift in cultural mores:

- "Sex offender arrested for murder kept online blog"
- "More teens experimenting with heroin"
- "Gay 'civil unions' approved by courts"
- "Terrorist warnings extended to rural areas"
- "Abducted girls posted address on Web site"
- "Mother who left toddler in car arrested"

Although we cannot allow today's shocking news headlines to paralyze us into locking our children away from any and all possibly perceived catastrophes, we should remain vigilant concerning the potential dangers our tweens face. Keeping a proper, loving grip on our tweens involves several safety procedures that must not be ignored. Parents today who disregard these precautions may reason, *These weren't required when I was a kid.* But, I repeat, times change. We may assume the best of others and hope that no evil touches our families, but safe parents follow these practices:

- Have a DNA or dental identification kit completed;
- Know where your tween is at all times;
- Know the phone numbers of her principal, teachers, and coaches;
- Investigate the history of the Web sites and chat rooms your tween frequents and never allow your tween access to a computer in private;
- Discuss problems occurring at school or in the neighborhood;
- Always know who's driving and who will (or won't) be around;
- Follow up on extreme mood swings or angry outbursts.

Take a Day Off Work

Some parents mistakenly believe taking time off to spend with their tweens will harm their careers. Studies demonstrate, however, that parents who care for their children's social and intellectual development are more likely to advance in their occupations.[7]

Our children grow up so quickly. One work day after another can pile up like yesterday's newspapers. We intend to take a day off to spend with our tweens, but the days turn to months and our tweens quickly becomes teens. Without the habit already established of spending time with family, there's probably a fifty-fifty chance our children would rather engage in an activity with their friends than spend an evening with one of their parents.

Parents who actively engage their tweens at deep emotional and spiritual levels spend quality *and* quantity time with their children. Your tween will love you for scheduling time away from work to spend with her. It will actually give you a double reward. Your tween will not only look forward to the time, but you can use those moments to connect on a deeper level not available during the daily grind.

Tune In to Your Tween

For several years I was a morning announcer at a Christian radio station in the Midwest. I never outgrew the amazement of sitting alone in a room and talking with thousands of listeners in their homes, cars, and worksites. I was always fascinated by the brave engineers who climbed the sky-high towers and repaired the satellite signals. It was their job to make sure that the station's signal was sent properly and that the intended audience could receive the feed.

If you're not doing so already, what would it mean to finely *tune in* to your tween's personal radio station signal? Like all humans, tweens must communicate. Whether they are laughing, screaming, or moping, our tweens are emitting a strong, communicative signal that we must learn to receive.

One of the harmful ways some parents tend to undercontrol and disengage from their children is by ignoring this constant and steady stream of communication. The inability or failure of some parents to tune in to their tweens may be purely accidental. There are a myriad of reasons why parents may be disconnected from their tweens' signal. These parents may be too busy, angry, or depressed. But the disconnection, over time, will cause distorted and damaged parental engagement patterns to set in.

Preadolescents are truly hurt by insensitive parents who don't turn on their "radios" and listen to the feelings their tweens are broadcasting. Over time these kids may simply give up hope of ever connecting, and stop broadcasting. Or they may choose to ignore those closest to them and broadcast to someone—anyone—who will pick up on their signals. This leaves them vulnerable to any number of harmful situations.

A Checklist

Finding the balance between allowing your tween safe self-exploration and unfettered freedom isn't easy. Here are a few areas in which there can be no compromise:

- Visit your child at school—either to eat lunch with or to visit him in the classroom.
- Know what your tween is reading.
- Know what your tween is viewing online.
- Know what music your tween listens to, including the lyrics.
- Have a child identification kit completed, in case your tween is ever lost or abducted.
- Know your tween's friends well.

Overweight Tweens

Tweens are now facing high levels of obesity and related diseases. In 1999, for example, 13 percent of tweens were considered overweight, a number triple that of 1980 levels. These high levels of obesity bring a dramatic increase in Type 2 diabetes. Studies indicate that an overweight tween will continue to be overweight or obese as an adult and will therefore carry an increased risk of heart disease, stroke, and cancer.[8]

Since you're reading this book and have read this far, you're probably a concerned, involved parent. You're probably the type of parent who wants to raise a world-class kid. And staying informed is an important step.

You are to be commended for studying these pages and thinking through how you can become a more effective parent. But no book, no expert can define for you the appropriate boundaries for your tween. Only God can give us the wisdom, grace, and faith to make it to the parenting finish line. You'll need, then, to continually think and pray through what rules and regulations are appropriate for your preadolescent.

Too Much or Too Little?

I love golf. The grip is one of the most important aspects of the golf swing. A grip that is too tight causes so much tension in the hands and arms during the swing that the hands do not "release" the club head properly. A grip that's too loose causes the golfer to lose control at the top of the back swing, which results in the player not knowing where the club head is during impact.

I think you know where I'm headed: the golf grip is analogous to our parenting styles. If our grip on our tweens is too tight, we cause way too much tension in our homes and in our children, and they become defensive. If, on the other hand, our parenting style is too loose, one of disengagement or abandonment, we don't know where our tweens "are at," and they're always testing boundaries, continually asking, *Who's really in charge around here?*

Balanced parenting requires that we constantly consider how our children are growing physically, emotionally, relationally, and spiritually—that is, as *whole* individuals. In addition, this style of parenting requires that we pay close attention to the manner in which we are releasing our children to explore their own individuality. We must remain equally sensitive to their desires to remain small children and cling to the safety and comforts of home, as well as honoring their newfound adolescent desire to go into the world and become their own persons.

As we ask ourselves whether we are the type of parent who practices too much or too little control, we need to consider several factors. First, ask yourself if the culture has changed, making it unsafe for your tween to freely play, roam, and discover. Second, is your child mature enough to handle the freedoms you desire for her? And third, how mature are the other children your tween associates with?

Children desire to know their own limits and boundaries. Tweens, of course, challenge these limits on what may seem like a daily basis. But subconsciously, they know they can't yet handle the added responsibilities that adolescence brings. Tweens are not ready for dating, saving for college, or providing for their own food and clothing.

As a parent, you have been chosen by God to lead your family. You are the one that will set vision and direction for your tween. Although they may loudly claim the contrary, they are always looking to you for love and limits. So don't be afraid to lead your tween. Discuss with your spouse what you believe to be reasonable and responsible limits. And then be confident in your enforcement of these rules and regulations.

The interesting result is that your child, more often than not, will follow your lead. If you believe your child needs to lose weight, invite him to go jogging with you. Wish your child spent more time in Bible reading or prayer? Spend time in prayer and Bible study with him. Whether or not you know it, your child is watching you like a hungry kid at a free candy counter.

Tweens Bombarded by Sexualized Cultural Forces

Twelve-year-olds are now being sold the same clothing line as eighteen-year-olds, says clinical psychologist Catherine Steiner-Adair, who works with adolescent girls. "We've really lost what used to be called the middle school years. It's almost like kids go from elementary school to teenagers. There's no pause," says Steiner-Adair. Noting that girls from nine to twelve are constantly bombarded with ads and images for push-up bras, thong underwear, eyeliner and mascara, bare bellies, and low-rider jeans, she adds, "It's turning girls into sexualized objects at an earlier age. . . . As a culture, we're selling sex to girls at a younger and younger age."[9]

Implement Real Change

Now comes the difficult part. You've prayed, and talked with your spouse, your own tween, and your friends. Everyone confirms you have a couple of specific problem areas. Now, what are you planning on doing to improve your parenting skills? Will this book only serve to make you aware of what tweens are going through as they mature and become their own persons? Or will you take the next step and implement a new parenting skill?

Change is difficult, but keep reminding yourself of the positive outcomes. Dream and pray about where you can improve in connecting with your tween. Remember what it was like when you were eight to twelve years old. Think back to what you most wanted at that time from your parents. It was probably affirmation, acceptance, or affection. And while it's impossible for you to turn back the clock, you can grow and develop as a parent as you provide these critically important developmental areas of growth for your own child.

Chapter Review

- Children need and want boundaries. If you don't provide them, you're exasperating your children.

- Today's tweens are being treated as yesterday's teens. Immerse yourself in tween culture and find out exactly what is being marketed to your tween and why.

- Examine your work schedule to be sure your tween is receiving both quality and quantity time.

- Your tween is constantly broadcasting feelings. If you ignore those broadcasts, you will leave him vulnerable to outside influences.

- Children are not born with blank moral slates. They are born with fallen sin natures and therefore need both love and limits.

Chapter Discussion Questions

1. Why would advertisers and marketers want to treat today's tweens as teens?

2. As you've studied this book and thought through the issues, what are some of the cultural differences between your tween years and your child's?

3. If a particular set of parents had little or no reasonable boundaries set for them as an example to emulate, how would they know where to begin with their own children?

4. Look at your schedule. Are you spending both quality and quantity time with your preadolescent? Are there some specific days or hours you could take off work to spend time with your tween? Could your tween visit you at work?

5

Why Authentic Communication with Your Tween Is Critical

This Chapter's Big Idea

It is vitally important that parents engage in authentic, heart-to-heart communication with their tweens during this normal developmental stage of exploration. But it is often enormously difficult for us to bridge the gap and engage in authentic communication with our tweens. Knowing the reasons behind the gap is important in building the bridge.

> Higher levels of father involvement in activities with their children—such as eating meals together, helping with homework, and going on family outings—has been found to be associated with fewer child behavior problems, higher levels of sociability, and higher levels of academic performance in children and adolescents.[1]

Talking vs. Communicating

Talking and communicating are two entirely different undertakings. When I was young, the Charles Schultz comic strip *Peanuts* was growing increasingly popular. When the strip moved from newsprint to television and began airing as animated movie specials, the characters each found his or her own voice. Everyone had his or her own distinct dialect and unique voice inflection, which accurately matched his or her personality and temperament—everyone, that is, except the adults.

If you'll remember, the schoolteacher had a voice of her own, but it made no sense—it did not communicate. To understand the voice of the schoolteacher, the viewer was forced to listen closely and follow along with the dialogue of the students. That's because we assume the teacher's mouth and lips were moving but the only sound emerging was a muffled, nonsensical, "wah-wah-wah-wah . . . wah-wah-wah-wah." If you remember the shows, this probably brings a smile. It was a funny device.

But this is also how our own tweens begin to hear us. During toddlerhood, our words as parents carried real weight. If we announced a stove was "hot!" or a knife was "sharp," our young children learned to believe us—or suffer the painful consequences. At the age of two, our children began questioning everything we said. Between the ages of eight and twelve, the questioning becomes perpetual and not always verbalized.

In the beginning, we parents were our children's main sources of interpersonal communication. We clucked and cooed along with every sound they uttered, and we recorded their undistinguishable mumbling and played it back for family and friends. We were proud to hear our kids communicating, and longed for deeper levels of interaction. Then they began talking with everyone—and everything.

As children discover peers, learn to communicate with adults, and ramble on to whomever or whatever will listen, the uniqueness of their communication becomes commonplace, even frustrating. It seems we spend the first two years trying to force our children to speak and the next two encouraging them to be quiet. Then as they begin entering their tween years, we may find ourselves again wishing our children would communicate with us.

I'm sure you'd confirm you spend plenty of time talking with your tween, maybe encouraging her to talk to you. But how much time do you spend really communicating? Do you actually "hear" your tween when you're communicating? Do you know the strong desires of her heart? Do you understand her grandest dreams and deepest fears? Do you grow "elephant ears" around your tween—giant ears that listen not only to unique sounds but individual feelings and emotions your tween emits on a moment by moment basis?

I love the story recorded by the gospel writer Mark of an incident that occurred while Jesus was walking amongst a crowd of people (5:24–34). A woman, who had spent all of her money seeing multiple doctors in an attempt to deal with a twelve-year-old bleeding problem, approached Jesus in a large crowd. We can imagine the near mob was shoulder to shoulder and possibly jostling each other. The woman is portrayed as having enough faith to reason, *If I just touch his clothes, I will be healed.*

When she was finally able to come up behind Jesus and touch his cloak, her bleeding stopped immediately, and she could feel in her body that her suffering had ceased. This incident is miracle enough on its own. What happened next, though, is equally intriguing. Mark records that Jesus spun around *in the crowd* and asked, "Who touched my clothes?" The disciples, Jesus' closest followers, were dumbfounded. They asked rhetorically, "We're in the midst of a mob here. We're packed in like sardines, and yet you ask 'Who touched me?'"

Are we this sensitive in our parenting efforts? Do we really pay attention when our children reach out to us? How many times have I ignored my children's heartfelt cries for attention?

In the womb, your child was one with his mother. Then during the first few weeks and months of life outside the womb, things slowly began to change. His own fingers came into view (*hmm*, tasty). He began to notice when he was being held and more importantly when he was not! (They do *tell* you, don't they?)

For a time, a child's life consists only of two worlds—"mother" and "not mother." But over time, other persons and things emerge in her life in addition to "mama." New objects come into consciousness: a father (dada), a family kitty cat (*ooh*, fluffy), and other adults (scary!).

This process of self-discovery has repeated itself over and over as an ongoing cycle of normal development. Well, hello, and welcome to preadolescence. Here we go all over again as this same self-discovery and separation process repeats itself.

But there is one major difference. Up to this point, you've been the authoritative center of your child's universe. He's looked to you for a description of who he is, what he's good at, and how he fits into the world outside. Now, subtly, he's looking not to you but to others for that same special insider information. He's viewing television, listening to music, and watching movies asking, *Where do I fit in with each of these stories?* and *Do I believe them to be true?*

Your tween will continue to check in with you—insofar as you've been accurate and she trusts you—but now she will progressively check in with other adults such as coaches, teachers, and religious leaders to tell her who she is.

So how do you insure that you've created a solid foundation for your tween's self-identity? How do you make sure that he will stay emotionally connected to you—and willing to check in with you—as a teen? The key is how well you authentically communicate with your tween now.

Creating an Accepting Home

The first step to creating an environment for authentic communication is helping your tween feel warmly accepted and fully validated in your home. One sure way is to lovingly invest in your child by telling her that you're proud of her, you accept her, you love her. These declarations are critical because the stakes are much higher now that she is desperately searching for these same affirmative messages of self-validation from trusted adults and her own circle of peers. If she feels dangerously isolated from you, she's left to struggle with the sometimes dangerous undertow from her friends and the surrounding culture.

As seasoned adults, we can attest to the truth that the outside world may or may not be as accommodating as the warmth and security of home. (Depends on what type of home you grew up in.) But this fact cannot be ignored—your tween is now entering the sometimes harsh world of peer-based reality.

The message now continually coursing through his mind is, *Am I accepted here? Am I cool? Do I fit in . . . do I belong?* Items as seemingly unimportant as shoes begin to take on significance equal to a presidential election. Your child wonders, *Do these shoes make me look cool? What do my friends think of my shoes? Are my shoes as cool as my friends' shoes?*

Suicide Warning Signs

Each year, almost five thousand young people, ages fifteen to twenty-four, kill themselves, making suicide the third leading cause of death among adolescents and the second leading cause of death among college-age youth. Four out of five teens who attempt suicide have given clear warnings. Pay attention to these:

- Suicide threats, direct and indirect
- Obsession with death
- Poems, essays, and drawings that refer to death
- Dramatic change in personality or appearance
- Irrational, bizarre behavior
- Overwhelming sense of guilt or shame
- Strange eating or sleeping patterns
- Severe drop in school performance
- Giving away belongings[2]

As mature (think *older*) adults, we reason from a much different framework. You and I reason, *Are these shoes comfortable? Are they a good buy? Do they have sturdy soles?* But in a real sense, as full-grown adults, we're through being cool. Not tweens . . . they're just getting warmed up. And you are there to assure her that she matters, no matter what kind of shoes she wears. But you can't "be there" if you don't know where "there" is. And that leads us to the second step of bridging the gap between you and your child.

Blocks to Authentic Communication

We all likely agree that ongoing, authentic, heartfelt communication is vital to our tweens' healthy development. Your efforts toward parenting your tween now will affect what your teen will do when peers announce, *There's nothing wrong with smoking marijuana . . . virginity is for losers . . . stealing is fun.*

But communicating with your tween doesn't often come naturally. As mentioned earlier, parents often spend the first two years encouraging their children to talk and the next two years trying to get them to be quiet. What that popular wisdom misses is that as a parent of a tween, you'll again find yourself wishing that your child would truly talk with you.

It may seem that at one moment you could easily discuss things with your child and then the next, she's on an entirely different continent speaking an entirely different language. The bad news is that you and your tween are headed toward a potential problem. More and more you'll experience difficulty in communicating. But here's the good news: you can work to become an ambassador to your teen. You just have to start now. And you have to recognize the reasons for this coming disconnect.

Unfamiliarity with Tween-speak

The first and most important reason for disconnect is that while your tween is going through this process of separation/individuation, you and she are beginning to speak two separate languages. That is, you're seeing the world through two different lenses or vantage points. We hope that we see the world through the eyes of a more grounded, responsibility-based parenthood. We often talk of love and limits, of rules and regulations, of curfews and bedtimes.

Our tweens, on the other hand, are busy exploring an exciting new world of endless possibilities. We could label this new life-stage "I'm almost a teenager now, and I will do things differently than when you were one." Perhaps he will grow up to become a professional athlete, an astronaut, or a Hollywood star. Then again, perhaps he won't. In any case, he doesn't have much use for our parental warnings of eating right, studying hard, and bathing frequently.

As tweens, our children now believe the sky is the limit and our frequent communication patterns, which attempt to bring them back down to earth, are like pins bursting their fantasy bubbles. You've probably seen the funny poster:

Attention Teenagers!

> If you are tired of being continually bothered and endlessly hassled by overbearing, unreasonable parents, now is the time for action! Move out and begin paying your own way now while you still know everything!

Dr. Henry Cloud and Dr. John Townsend wrote about this problem in their best-seller *Boundaries: When to Say Yes, When to Say No, to Take Control of Your Life.* In a section on allowing others the freedom to suffer the results of their own behavior, Cloud and Townsend remind us,

> Parents often yell and nag, instead of allowing their children to reap the natural consequences of their behavior. Parenting with love and limits, with warmth and consequences, produces confident children who have a sense of control over their lives.[3]

Parenting expert Dr. James Dobson provides similar counsel when he warns,

> Parents often use anger to get action instead of using action to get action. . . . Trying to control children by screaming is as utterly futile as trying to steer a car by honking the horn.[4]

Our children often believe they are ready to take on more responsibility than they can handle, and it shows in their somewhat awkward communications. Maybe you've heard the funny line from the highly independent seven-year-old. He announced to his mother and father at the dinner table, "Okay, that's it. I've had it! I'm running away from home tomorrow morning! Now, which one of you is going to drive me?"

You can easily see how simple communication becomes muddled. In our attempt to show our tweens how much we care for them by providing legitimate warnings and pronouncements of advice, we often come across as speaking a harsh language our tweens easily dismiss or tune out.

Although effective communication is transactional in nature—with both the receiver and the sender involved in the process—our *parent talk* is often one-way. Many well-meaning parents do most of the talking and very little of the listening. I often ask myself, "Do I fall into this camp?"

The following is an example of poor "parent-talk" communication:

PARENT.   I sometimes wonder whether or not you really appreciate just how hard your mother and I work to provide for you and your needs. Do you think it's easy working every day and trying to save money to pay all of the bills around here? When I was your age I was shoveling snow from driveways in the winter and mowing lawns in the summer! You only have one or two chores, which you skip half the time, and yet you want us to take you to the mall and buy you new jeans?

TWEEN.   Well, I was just . . .

PARENT.   And it wasn't just snow I shoveled. I use to work at old Mr. Neukirch's farm and he had me shoveling out the horse stalls when I was younger than you! I used to get out there at the crack of dawn and work all day in the hot sun. I was lucky if I got one new pair of jeans for the start of school!

TWEEN.   It's my money . . . I was just thinking . . .

PARENT.   Let me tell you what old Mr. Neukirch taught me about money! You wanna talk about money. He taught me . . . and he had a bunch of money . . . old Mr. Neukirch did! He taught me the best way to double my money was to fold it in half and put it back in my pocket! I haven't seen you saving your money!

Tweens Influence Purchasing Decisions

Thanks to allowances, birthday money, generous grandparents, and other sources, tweens have a significant disposable income that is now rivaling that of their boomer parents. Sociologists now report that tweens are very vocal about the family car, what food the family buys, and where they want the family to go for vacation. Recent statistics show that over 60 percent of tween boys make their own fast food choices and over 70 percent of boys and girls at age thirteen make their own clothing choices. Car manufacturers now believe that boys under ten know what car they want to drive when they graduate to driving status.[5]

If you're smiling, it's probably a painful smile of recognition. In this particular communication transaction, only the parent is "heard." The tween has no real voice. Also, the parent is not listening to the tween's heart but is instead judging and assigning value based on information that is not even originating from the tween. The following is an example of the transactional, authentic communication style advocated in this book:

PARENT.   Heard you want some new jeans?

TWEEN.   Yeah, but you probably won't take me to the store!

PARENT.   Oh really, what makes you think so?

TWEEN.   Okay, c'mon, let's go to the mall right now!

PARENT.   All right, take a deep breath, and let's talk. Why do you want new jeans?

TWEEN.   Mine are way out of style. I want the cool ones everyone has!

PARENT.   Oh, has everyone in your class got the cool, new jeans?

TWEEN.   Um . . . no . . . not really, but Tina has.

PARENT.   Hmm, I didn't know you wanted new jeans. I thought you were saving your money for that purse that you just had to have.

TWEEN.   Well, yeah, that too. I want to get the purse but I also want to get the jeans. Then I'll have everything I want.

PARENT.   I'm proud of the way you've been saving your money. This reminds me of the way your dad and I have to decide on buying things around here. Remember last winter? We wanted to get the new car . . . but we wanted the whole family to go skiing too.

TWEEN.   Oh, yeah! I totally forgot about not going on the ski trip. I'm glad we got the new car instead! Our old car was embarrassing!

PARENT.   Well, we can go tomorrow and use your "purse" money to buy the jeans if you want, but then you'd have to save for a while to get the purse too.

TWEEN.   Hmm . . .

In this conversation the parent is actively listening and seeking to understand the tween. This parent (1) asked discerning questions to get at the heart of the matter, (2) didn't lecture or scold, (3) listened to what the daughter was expressing (and you'll note that the parent also remembered information from a previous conversation), and (4) offered alternatives in an attempt at finding a middle way.

Not Slowing Down Long Enough to Hear the Differences

Another reason communication is strained between parent and tween is that the two camps are so busy. Many parents are rushed and many tweens are, too. Let's face facts: Americans, in general, are on the go. Don't believe me? Let's bring this idea out of the realm of the theoretical and into the highly practical. When was the last time you had a lengthy, uninterrupted conversation of substance with your tween when you both communicated from the heart about important issues like friends, his future, or life in general? If it's been a while I strongly urge you to literally make an appointment, carve out the time, and spend some time talking with your tween.

Every once in a while it happens at our house by accident. Say the electricity goes out or we all arrive home from a special event. Everyone is in a celebratory mood and we're normally arranged in some sort of circle. Maybe it's a birthday gathering or important milestone someone's just reached. In any event, we start having a good time unencumbered by outside influences like the constant drone of mindless television or the worries of tomorrow's daily grind.

In those moments, our family hums like a well-maintained Indy 500 race car; we hit on all cylinders. Everyone encourages one another. We give and take good, solid advice. We laugh and crack jokes. We smile. We enjoy. Time stands still. In those moments when the planets seem to align, we realize that being a part of the Pettit family is the best place on Earth.

During these times, when everyone is relaxed and being themselves, I notice subtle differences in each of our family members. Some are louder and more outward-oriented than others. Some are more reserved, preferring to let others lead the way. But each is distinct, with his or her own fingerprint of personality. Most biblical scholars believe Proverbs 22:6 teaches each child should be trained *according to his own unique way.* Charles Swindoll writes,

Each child is hand-stitched by the Lord—not mass-manufactured in some sweatshop. For instance, the mind is intricately woven with the finest of neurological threads. The emotions are given a distinct texture, with a feel all their own. The personality is cut from a unique bolt of cloth . . . no two are alike.[6]

Like me, you may have poured over parenting books that advocate "these specific steps" or "this proven theory." I've found each of my own children to be vastly different from the others. With one, spanking works wonders. With another, a stern look brings a quivering lip. No cookie-cutter style seems to do the trick. And would we really want it any other way?

When I'm in a hurry, however, when my parenting efforts seem rushed, it feels as though any old style will work. When my wife and I are awfully busy, when life is moving at the speed of the twenty-first century, it takes real effort and premeditation to slow down and seek out the wonderful differences in our amazing children.

Differences in the way kids communicate reminds me of two mothers of teenagers who were catching up at the grocery store. The first mom admitted, "My daughter doesn't tell me *anything*; I'm a nervous wreck!" The second mom revealed, "My daughter tells me *everything*, and I'm a nervous wreck!"

Authentically communicating with our tweens can be daunting, but the process is critically important. Every time we slow down long enough to embrace the divine differences, my kids tell me amazing things they're thinking and dreaming about for their own futures.

More often than not, living with a tween can be a barrel of fun, despite what Mark Twain is purported to have said. His advice for parenting teenagers went something like this: When a child turns thirteen, place him in a barrel, nail the lid shut, and feed him through a knothole. When he turns sixteen, plug the knothole.

Angry Tweens

Another reason why communication between parent and tween is strained may involve some hurt or pain that is affecting the process, clogging the lines of interaction. My son or daughter may not feel like speaking honestly with me because he or she has been offended or hurt by something I may have said or done.

The next time you sense some emotional distance between you and your tween, ask him a difficult but highly effective question: *Have I said or done anything lately that has hurt your feelings?* Then be prepared to listen. Don't defend yourself and don't lecture. Take a deep breath and try to see things from your tween's perspective. More often than not, he will have a legitimate concern that you can easily address together.

Once you've heard him out, you may need to explain yourself, you may need to apologize, and you may need to change. In communicating at deep levels with your tween you might be surprised at what you learn. We may be unaware of the little offenses we have committed against our children in the past. In fact they may appear as no big deal to us. And yet to our children they were devastating. These offenses, continually repeated over time, can cause our children to develop a "root of bitterness" against us. Our children can become angry over these past hurts and tune us out.

It's important that we clear the air on a regular basis while our tweens are exploring their own identities. Anger always serves as a block to authentic communication. The apostle Paul warned, "Do not let the sun go down while you are still angry, and do not give the devil a foothold" (Eph. 4:26 NIV). Further, he specifically warned dads, "Do not provoke your children to anger" (Eph. 6:4.). A wonderful guide to authentic communication is provided by the apostle James who counseled, "Everyone should be quick to listen, slow to speak and slow to become angry" (James 1:19 NIV).

Authentic communication conveys the notion of parents and tweens making a heartfelt connection. During this time of change and transition into adolescence and ultimately adulthood, these barriers to effective communication must be scaled. I'm convinced I do my best parenting when I'm in listening mode more than when I'm in speaking mode. And I know I'm not parenting well when I'm in foaming-at-the-mouth-and-yelling mode.

Age Differences

That parents and tweens do not communicate well because their ages are so far apart may seem obvious, but it's not normally discussed. We sometimes take it for granted that our tweens have been through all of the same life experiences we've been through. Obviously most parents of tweens are in their thirties, forties, or fifties. We may forget that our children have not experienced many of the same milestones we have. They have never driven a car, enrolled in a college course, probably have not sat for a job interview, or received a regular paycheck. And yet we often expect that they should fully understand each of these life stages. And we even treat them as if they have experienced them.

The age gap makes authentic communication difficult at times. We've lived twenty-five to thirty-five years longer than our tweens. We've learned many life lessons we need to pass on, but our tweens cannot learn them during one angry outburst or one teaching session at summer camp. As we practice authentic communication with our tweens, it's helpful to remove our age-colored lenses and see life as a tween sees it.

We've all heard the jokes about older people telling younger people how it was in the "good old days." We all break into a smile when we hear an experienced parent or grandparent start a minilecture with those famous words, "Why, when I was your age . . ." These stories normally entail descriptions of walking to school in a blizzard or waking at five AM to perform back-breaking chores. We smile at those stories, but we sometimes tune them out as well. Despite our life-experience stories holding great teaching value, they can easily become "good old days" stories to our tweens.

We can communicate clearly and authentically by beginning, "Okay, you're right. I'm forty-three and you're eleven. I'll tell you what it was like when I was your age, and then you tell me what it was like at school today." We can break through age differences and make heartfelt connections when we're committed to parenting well and remain aware of communication breakdowns.

Cultural Changes

Cultural differences inhibit authentic communication in a way similar to age differences. Just as we are different ages, and therefore have more life experience than our tweens, we also lived during a different cultural period in history as well. At different times in recent history, cultural norms prevailed. At one time, children were expected to be seen and not heard. It was considered improper for girls to call boys on the phone. When a girl entered a room, a boy was to stand and remove his cap as a sign of respect. And the neighbors were always addressed as Mr. and Mrs. Smith.

Think about your tween and her friends. If your tween is anything like mine, she is heard loud and clear, girls instant message boys, my boys seem to have their ball caps sewn into their scalps, and the neighbors are known casually as Chris and Heather.

Obviously you can see how these cultural differences contribute to a breakdown in authentic communication. It can be difficult to share heart-to-heart times with our tweens if they are unclear of our expectations and what we consider to be normal, polite standards of behavior. I often catch myself needing to slow down and spell out exactly *why* I hold to a particular belief or value. Remember that during this period your child is questioning everything. If you give him the whys to your values, he is more likely to adopt those values as his own.

The book of Exodus begins by declaring, "Now a new king arose over Egypt, who did not know Joseph." What was true of Pharaoh could be said about our tweens as well. They may not know many of the stories about your grandparents, which you take for granted. They may have never heard or really understood how hard you used to work or how difficult school was for you. They probably haven't thought much about how culture has changed since you were a tween. Allow these differences to spark your communication sessions.

Styles and Technologies

Another barrier to authentic communication includes the enormous technological changes our society has undergone. I recently heard of a mother who e-mailed her son to tell him dinner was ready—and he was upstairs in his bedroom! Fax machines, cell phones, instant messaging, pagers—all of these can either help or hinder authentic communication.

I may have a strong desire to communicate with my tween, and yet I need to study her communication styles and patterns to insure I'm making a connection. Parents and tweens can exist on two different frequencies, thinking they are communicating, but hearing only static. In a much earlier time, children sat and listened to orally communicated stories. Another era saw children and families huddled around radios, listening to dramas and comedies. Many of today's parents can recall sitting in living rooms, watching television with friends and family members.

Tweens in Touch with the World

Tweens today have greater opportunities to reach out to peers both near and far. Today's preadolescents are the first generation to benefit from high-tech communication technologies like the Internet. "They are a savvy group that are already used to being able to communicate around the world," says Dr. Dan Wheeler, a researcher who specializes in educational technology. "It doesn't really sink in to them that they are the first group of kids to be able to do this so easily. What really impresses me about this age group is how kids are taking to this new electronic world and are becoming part of a global culture."[7]

In today's technology explosion, it seems everyone in the family can be wearing his or her own set of headphones, listening to music, phone calls, sports shows, or news—and they're all in the same car! Monitor your messages and see if you're actually communicating with your tween. Ask her often if she would like to talk or simply begin a conversation with the intent of listening deeply.

Trying Out Identities

Why is authentic communication so vitally important during this phase? Your tween needs a safe place where he can ask questions, explore new ideas, and try out new behaviors. If you shut down and avoid discussing these issues with him, he'll become confused, having no compass by which to navigate the options. He needs a steady, true north to guide him so he can safely explore the outside world. This phase of development is like a dance of exploration. Your tween will move out into the world and back in to his family, back and forth, as he tries out new identities, then discusses them in the home.

One day your tween may, for example, spend the afternoon studying and announce he's dreaming about attending an Ivy League university. And then, only a couple of days later, this same tween may spend all morning involved in a video game while calmly explaining that instead of college he's thinking of devoting his life to working full-time at the surfboard shop.

This bouncing around may drive you to seek out a professional career counselor. But his trying out new career ideas is a quite normal behavior for a tween. Remember he's separating from you. At those times when he feels most secure and most loved, he also feels most like trying to reach the outer limits of who he is becoming as a person. So when he feels most safe, he feels most like leaving because he knows he has a home base to which he can return if needed.

At the same time, your tween is also individuating. So when life in your home becomes highly routine and patterned, she most feels like stretching her new self-image and trying her own new routines and patterns. Let's say you're a physician, and your father was a physician. Know how predictable that feels to your tween? So when your father sits your daughter down at Thanksgiving and asks what she sees for herself in her future, you won't be surprised when she announces she's anxious to get started in her career as a stunt fighter-pilot.

Presidential Ambitions

Most eleven- to thirteen-year-olds say they have no desire to be the President of the United States.

Kids who want to be the USA's CEO: Yes—43 percent; No—57 percent[8]

Both separation and individuation are normal developmental patterns that follow attachment. Remember, your infant separated and individuated from the oneness that described his relationship with his mother. Now he's exploring what it will be like once he's completely out on his own. And you get to be there to walk him through this exciting discovery. In that sense, you're his tour guide into adulthood. You can portray the upcoming responsibilities to him as foreboding and dark—*Oooh there's adulthood just around the corner; look out!*—or as the normal, next stage of life to be encountered and enjoyed. You can become exasperated when your tween initiates stops that are not on the tour agenda, or you can use them as teaching moments. It's all in how you approach the trip.

Inside a neighborhood supermarket a man pushed a cart, which contained a screaming baby. The gentleman kept repeating softly, "Don't get excited, Albert. Don't scream, Albert. Don't yell, Albert . . . keep calm, Albert." A woman shopping next to him finally commented, "Well, you certainly are to be commended for trying to soothe Albert, your little son." The frazzled dad looked back at her and replied, "Ma'am, *I'm* Albert!" That young father was trying to avoid exasperation on his trip with his son. Which kind of tour guide are you?

Sometimes I wonder whether I'm raising my children or my children are raising me. Throughout the duration of our parenting journey, let's be open and flexible regarding the tremendous task God has laid before us. Besides, if our kids were perfect, how would we learn to trust God more? Just like any other task we undertake, we will never do this one perfectly. So let's relax. Take a deep breath. Enjoy the journey. Your kids will love you for your genuine flexibility, honest communication, and patient resilience.

Chapter Review

- It is dangerous for children to feel isolated and alone during the transitional tween years. Effective parents draw their children out with heart-to-heart conversation.

- While your tween is exploring the outside world, the world of ideas and philosophies outside of your home, you'll want to keep the lines of communication wide open. Schedule time with your tween. Ask questions early and often.

- There are many blocks to communicating with your tween including busyness, anger, age differences, cultural differences, and technology.

- Ask your child what her friends are discussing and talk about those topics with her. You may be surprised by what you'll learn.

Chapter Discussion Questions

1. What are the differences between talking and communicating?

2. What are some of the reasons why tweens begin to "tune out" the voices of their parents?

3. Discuss some of the blocks you experience when you try authentically communicating with your tween. What can you do to overcome these blocks?

4. Why would a tween who harbors anger in his heart find it difficult to communicate at deep levels? Does your tween have any issues he's angry about?

5. You may believe you and your tween communicate well. What would be a way to check if this is true?

6

Using Authentic
Communication
to Tune In to Your Tween

This Chapter's Big Idea

How do you tune in to your tween? You'll need to spend lots of unstructured time together, remain open and honest regarding any fears you may have about your tween or her future, and practice your tween's preferred style of communication.

> Train up a child in the way he should go,
> Even when he is old he will not depart from it.
> —Proverbs 22:6

The self-fulfilling prophecy operates in families as well. If parents tell a child long enough that he can't do anything right, his self-concept will soon incorporate this idea, and he will fail at many or most of the tasks he attempts. On the other hand, if a child is told that he is a capable or lovable or kind person, there is a much greater chance of his behaving accordingly.[1]

To review, the first key strategy advocated in this book was your using a balanced-parenting approach. Like a snapshot developing in your brain, a clearer picture of balanced parenting should by now be apparent. It doesn't matter whether you visualize this process as a seesaw on an elementary school playground, a sound golf swing, or a mother robin who makes her nest uncomfortable over time. The idea is to evaluate your parenting efforts by looking for activities or attitudes that may be out of balance and correcting those imbalances.

The second key strategy is spending both quality and quantity time with your tween in authentic communication. In order to understand the motives and desires of our preadolescents, we must get right up next to them and listen at deep levels; that is, we must learn to listen with our hearts. What is your tween's greatest fear, his greatest desire, his goals for the future? Do you know? Authentic communication must occur since your tween is so heavily involved in the developmental whirlwind of self-discovery and self-understanding.

Authentic Communication Requires Time: Both Quality and Quantity Time

Do you remember when you experienced your first real boyfriend or girlfriend? You were probably a teenager and not fully in control of your emotions. You may have spent endless nights on the phone with that person, discussing nothing in particular. More than likely you leisurely strolled with that person through a park blooming in the spring, and the hours sped by way too fast. You wanted to spend as much time together as possible. Life was good.

Imagine, however, that your special one came to you during these romantic days and announced, "I feel I should start spending more quality time with you and not quite as much quantity time." How do you think you would've felt about that? What if your "crush" further stated, "From now on, when we're together, I'd like to accomplish something . . . you know, tackle some project"? My guess is that your times together would cease to feel spontaneous and romantic.

Our tweens want to spend structured *and* unstructured time with us—bunches of it. In fact, tweens spell love, t-i-m-e. They desire both quality time and quantity time. Some misguided parental advocates have suggested that as long as parents spend various amounts of quality time with their children, they need not worry about spending quantity time. The truth is that while children are in the tween years, they need both quality and quantity time. Family researcher Dr. Ronald Levant has said,

> I think quality time is just a way of deluding ourselves into shortchanging our children. Children need vast amounts of parental time and attention. It's an illusion to think they're going to be on your timetable, and that you can say "OK we've got half and hour, let's get on with it."[2]

Preadolescents are headed for a difficult period of testing during which they will be forced to make many difficult decisions. We often leave our most lasting impressions in those moments when we may mistakenly believe that our children are not even watching us. Think about those times, for instance, when you happened to be in the company of your tween and something significant was passed along to her. Perhaps your tween witnessed you giving money back to a grocery store clerk who handed you too much change. Or your praying out loud because you were afraid or nervous.

Those were certainly quality-time moments that represented authentic communication, but were they planned? Your tween witnessed those moments simply because she was with you. Authentic communication can't take place, then, if we don't give our tweens the quantity time necessary.

Echoing these sentiments, Christian psychologist Dr. Kevin Leman writes,

> I frequently hear parents talking about "quality time." I understand what parents mean by that, but in all my years of private practice I've never heard one of my young clients (the children) mention "quality time." All a child knows is that he wants your time and your attention, whether it's to watch him do somersaults and cartwheels or to take him for a Big

Mac. . . . Give them all the time you can and the quality will take care of itself.[3]

Authentic Communication Requires Honesty and Openness

Practicing authentic communication with our tweens also requires honesty and openness on our part. I often find my children are more honest and open than I am. They're ready to discuss various issues that I may feel they're not yet ready, for whatever reason, to discuss. It is my nervousness or lack of openness, not theirs, that blocks authentic communication from occurring.

In a nationwide survey of fifth to eighth graders, seventy-three percent of kids say they spend less than one hour a day talking with their families. Only twenty percent said it's "very easy" to talk to parents about things that really matter. Twenty-six percent said it's "somewhat difficult" or "very difficult" to talk about serious topics with their parents.[4]

There's no way authentic communication is going to happen if you're not being honest with your tweens. You'll need to open up and practice authenticity and vulnerability yourself before you can expect it from your tweens.

Do you share your heart with your children when, for example, you're worried about how to pay the bills, or whether or not your paycheck is going to last until the end of the month? Or do you mistakenly believe that sharing this information with them will somehow scare them? It's necessary that you address any fears you have about communicating with your tween if you expect heartfelt communication to flow back and forth. I'm not advocating that you make your tweens feel responsible for making up the gap in the family budget. But if they're going to understand the real world, and understand why they can't have that new video game, they need to know what real life struggles look like.

In my work with graduate-school students, I coach small group leaders as they lead students who are going into full-time, vocational Christian ministry. As we place students into small groups, we ask them to practice authenticity and vulnerability with the other six or seven students in their small group. For some, this happens naturally. For others, the process of opening up and sharing from the heart is a real struggle. Why is this?

Some are afraid that if they open up and share the truth about their own lives others won't like them, or worse, will judge them and find them lacking. They are more interested in maintaining a certain image or preconceived notion of who they are rather than allowing others to see the real person inside. In our office our team labels this protective, defensive behavior "image management."

How tragic when you and I engage in these same defensive strategies in our parenting efforts. Instead of our tweens seeing the real us—people who have normal and natural struggles, people who struggle with pride, and doubt, and sin—we sometimes practice *parental image management* and act as if we have it all together.

How will your tween learn to deal with his issues and struggles if you don't show him the way? Again, this isn't to say you should scare him or overly burden him with your problems. But you will find that being vulnerable will allow him to open up to you.

Further, you and I may need to learn some new communication skills and strategies in order for us to communicate authentically with our tweens. If we find we're not connecting with our children the way we long to, we need to rethink our communication habits and tendencies. We may think our angry outbursts or our moments of awkward silence are having no effect. And yet, in our heart of hearts, we know better.

In communicating with your son or daughter, it's important not to minimize or dismiss what your tween is feeling. Here are seven communication strategies you can begin employing right away if you're not already doing so:

1.   Practice rephrasing what you hear your tween saying.

     Bad example:

     DAUGHTER.   I'm sick of going to family camp every summer. They treat us like babies there.

PARENT.   You just don't like having to stay with the
               counselors!

DAUGHTER.   Mom! You just don't understand!

Good example:

MOM.   Hmm, from what I hear you saying, the kids
               were really mean to you at school today.

DAUGHTER.   Oh no, they were just kidding, it was really
               funny.

MOM.   Oh, okay, I thought they were being serious.

2. Practice playing "high-low" around the dinner table.

    Bad example:

DAD.   Okay, let's all go around the table and tell what
               the best part of our day was and what the worst
               part was.

DAUGHTER.   I got to eat frozen yogurt at the mall. I love that
               stuff!

DAD.   How could that be the highlight of your day?
               Didn't you go to the zoo today?

Good example:

PARENT.   Let's all go around the table and tell what the
               best part of our day was and what the worst
               part was.

SON.   My high was phys ed class because I hit a home
               run during whiffle ball and the bases were
               loaded! But my low was science class because
               we dissected a pig and that was totally gross!

PARENT.   I don't think I'd like that job either! How did
               you do?

DAUGHTER.   My high was sitting on the bus on the way
               home because I sat right behind Craig Cooper

and he is way cute! My low was English class because I thought our research papers were due tomorrow, but they were due today!

PARENT.   That must have been quite a shock! How did you feel?

3. Work hard at making eye contact when talking with your tween. You may even need to physically get down on her level.

Bad example:

DAUGHTER.   Sally was with a bunch of other girls today, and when I said hi to her, she just turned her head away.

DAD.   Oh? That must have hurt your feelings. Hey, could you scoot over just a bit, I can't see the football game.

Good example:

DAUGHTER.   When Billy saw my new hair cut he said, "You look like somebody put a bowl over your head and cut around the edges!"

DAD.   Really? I can tell by the look on your face that what he said hurt your feelings. Why don't you click the off button on the TV remote and come sit by me on the couch? There. How do *you* feel about your new haircut?

4. Turn off the television and play a board game or some other family activity. Television normally inhibits family conversation.

5. Ask the "What's your favorite . . ." question throughout the day.

Bad example:

PARENT.   Okay, Evan, what was your favorite part of vacation Bible school today?

EVAN.   I would have to say break time. It was so hot outside today, it felt great to finally come indoors into the air conditioning.

PARENT.   Break time? No, I mean something like the Bible lesson or the praise and worship time during the puppets. How can you say break time was your favorite?

Good example:

MOM.   What was your favorite part about the soccer game today?

SON.   I liked it when they let me be the captain.

MOM.   Oh really, why was that?

SON.   Because our coach usually lets the captains do the kickoff at the start of the game.

MOM.   Aha, now I know why!

6. Take "talk-walks" together. It's almost impossible to remain silent during a walk.

7. Be a patient listener.

Bad example:

DAUGHTER.   Dad, did you hear I may be able serve in the concession stand at the softball games this summer? Okay, here's what happened—Mr. Jones said they need students to work at the games this summer . . . oh, and he also said—

DAD.   Just get to the bottom line, I don't need to hear all the details. Will you be getting paid or not?

Instead of interrupting your son or daughter, be patient and allow your tween to fully finish all sentences and wait until she's finished speaking before offering a response. Don't rush your tween to get to the point until she's ready.

Remember that invalidating your tween's response or putting him down because his response doesn't measure up to what you were expecting to hear discourages a tween from expressing his preferences, feelings, opinions, and thoughts in general.

The Blessing

Family relationship experts Dr. Gary Smalley and Dr. John Trent penned the best-seller, *The Blessing*. In it, they explain the Old Testament pattern parents used to honor their children and demonstrate unconditional acceptance. The five parts of the blessing include

1.   Meaningful touch.
2.   A spoken message.
3.   Attaching "high value" to the one being blessed.
4.   Picturing a special future for the one being blessed.
5.   An active commitment to fulfill the blessing.[5]

Authentic Communication Requires Understanding

It's impossible not to communicate. Whether someone screams, sits silently, or sighs with boredom, he's communicating nonetheless. As we parent our tweens and prepare to walk with them through their approaching stage of adolescence, it's critical we learn to listen to their hearts. Sure, words are important, but so are actions. You've heard the saying, "Your actions speak so loud I can't hear what you're saying." And we've all, of course, heard the proverb, "Actions speak louder than words."

Our children may be telling us one thing with their words, but their behaviors may belie their speech. Some of the best parenting advice I ever received urged that I continually ask questions when I'm with my children. I've tried to employ that strategy on a regular basis.

At dinnertime around the Pettit table, we invariably play a game we call high/low. About halfway through our evening meal, someone will suggest we play this discussion game, which allows each family member to share what both the high and the low point of his or her day involved. It's one small way we try to stay emotionally connected with our kids.

Another communication strategy I practice is to continually ask my children questions concerning what they like *best*. When riding home from a school event or sports practice, for example, I'll often ask, "What did you like best about practice today?" If my tween tells me that he or she liked kicking the ball best, I'll try to narrow down the source of that pleasure in an attempt to get at exactly what that tween enjoyed doing. "What did you like best about kicking the ball?" These types of clarifying questions get at your child's motivational patterns and help reveal what they're passionate about doing in life.

One child may announce, "I enjoyed kicking the ball because I got to the ball before Brooke did. Usually she gets all the goals, but today I kicked the ball into the goal!" Another child, after announcing what he enjoyed most about practice was "kicking the ball," may further clarify his answer by saying, "My coach told me I finally kicked the ball with my left foot!" These differing answers help us get at the hearts of our tweens and help us communicate with them at greater levels of authenticity and vulnerability.

Listening with the heart means carefully watching and closely observing our children so that we can better *understand* them. Why does one of my children want to read all of the time while another hates reading? Why does one love meeting new people and making new friends while another prefers being alone? Am I close enough to my children to really understand them? This is a parenting challenge each of us must tackle.

Authentic Communication Requires Listening with the Heart

Learning to listen with the heart requires ample doses of humility and patience. These are virtues many of us hold in short supply. I want to be an effective father, and I often know what I should do to pull off the task. And yet so often I blow it. I fail to engage my children in authentic communication. I don't listen with my heart, failing to engage my child with my full, undivided attention. I don't make eye contact and ask clarifying questions. On the ride home from practice, I'll listen to sports radio instead of tuning in to my child's true heart.

Learning to listen well involves humility because we often view our children's problems as less important than our own. I have important bills to pay. I have phone calls to return. I have to worry about the economy and the environment. Compared to this litany, my children's problems can seem trivial when, in fact, they are not. It takes humility to get on their emotional wavelength and tune in to what they're experiencing on a moment by moment basis because we are so often tuned in to our own emotional wavelength. Do I know who their friends are? Do I know their current struggles?

Learning to listen with the heart also takes patience because it may take time for my tweens to really open up and share what they're feeling. Too often I want to schedule time with my children in the expectation they'll be ready and willing to engage in heartfelt communication when *I* am ready for it. *It's Saturday morning. I've got a few minutes here. "Hey, Austin, what's on your heart right now?"* (Huh?) It takes practiced patience to listen and observe over a longer period of time in a genuine effort to understand my twelve-year-old.

Learning to listen with the heart also involves encouragement. I can't encourage accurately if I don't listen closely. Accurate encouraging is like when your friend, who knows how to throw a football well, stands beside you, coaching you on the process. *Okay, hold the football with your fingers along the laces . . . here, let me show you . . . like this. Good! That's much better. Now get ready to fling it . . . no . . . not from out to the side . . . but overhead like this. Are you ready . . . are you ready to throw it? Go ahead . . . try it!* A good friend will engage you in the process. He'll walk along with you as you experiment with a new task.

What kind of friend would laugh and ridicule us as we tried to learn a new hobby? *Oh, for heaven's sake, you call that throwing a football? It went straight down . . . my stars, you'll never learn!* No, we'd much rather hear a patient word of encouragement and understanding wouldn't we? *Oh man, now you're getting it! You got a good spin on it that time. You should have seen the first time I tried to throw a football. It landed on our roof . . . it took me forever to learn how to throw it!* Let's practice the parental art of authentic communication where we learn to "speak the truth in love."

Finally, learning to listen with the heart can be painful. Since we all try to avoid painful experiences, we sometimes begin to tune out our tweens because the secrets they share with us hurt. When I get down on one knee and get brutally honest with one of my children, they sometimes share information I'd rather not hear: "The kids in my class were mean to me today . . . they were teasing me and making fun of me"; "I wanted to talk with you yesterday, Daddy, but you just kept reading the newspaper." (Ouch . . . that hurts.)

Learning to listen with the heart takes patience, requires humility, and can be painful. But I cannot overemphasize how important the practice is and how well it prepares you and your tween for her journey into adolescence. If you're not experiencing authentic communication now, during the vulnerable tween years, don't think you'll suddenly start communicating at deep levels when your child is a teen and may be heading for trouble. It just doesn't work that way. It wasn't raining when Noah began building the ark.

Implementing authentic communication takes practice. It also takes discipline. You may need to unplug some electronic devices and tune out much of the busyness that enters into your normal routine. Proverbs 20:5 reveals, "The purposes of a man's heart are deep waters, but a man of understanding draws them out" (NIV). Your tween's heart is like a deep well. He is currently mulling over who he is and what his future plans look like. Communicating authentically with him is like knocking at the door of his heart and being allowed to enter.

Why is it so important that we practice communicating well with our tweens as they move through the preadolescent developmental phases? Isn't it enough to provide food, shelter, and clothing for them as we pursue our own dreams? As they move back and forth, searching for their authentic selves, they will open themselves to outside influences, which may or may not be in their best interests.

Tweens are inside of what one family researcher called a "sensitive period."[6] They are highly sensitive to suggestions as to who they are and what they should become. And since they are still assigned to you—still under your watchful care—it is your responsibility, your duty, your *joy*, to be able to speak most directly into their lives.

As the four of you (you, God, your spouse, and your tween) involve yourselves in this dance of parenting, real change is occurring. Your child is exploring what it means to be more like you and less like you. At times, your child may want to become a little more like her dad and a little less like her mother. And then, a little less like her dad and a little more like her mother. Siblings are involved, as well as friends and other outside observers and participants. Teachers and neighbors, movie stars and radio announcers, political figures and writers are all vying for her time and attention. But at least at this stage, you still have the most to say. Yours is still the most authoritative voice.

Soon that voice will change to that of your tween's peers. So use your voice well. Use your voice after you use your ears, and you will be communicating authentically from the heart. Watch and listen and learn. Be prepared to *speak into* or address his situation when his dance of engagement/estrangement spins him back into your arms.

Fold him in, speak truth in love, and then send him back out to a
watching and waiting world. God gave us two ears and one mouth,
so let's listen twice as much as we speak.

Frisbee Parenting

Engaging your child in authentic communication and allowing
her to explore who she is during her tween years is a little bit like
throwing a Frisbee. First you hold the Frisbee close to your side with
your arm coiled in and around the flying disc, almost as if the Frisbee is enfolded in your arm, a part of you. This is a picture of the
infant years, when parents and baby are in a symbiotic relationship.
Next, you make several motions with your arm, first holding the
Frisbee at arm's length and then coiling it back toward you, back
and forth, gauging how hard and at what height you plan on releasing the disc. This could be viewed as the preadolescent years, in
which tweens try on differing personas. Finally, one final coiling of
the arm and whoosh, the flying disc is released. This is a picture of
your young adult leaving home and heading into the world.

The funny part about throwing a Frisbee is the difficulty of properly releasing the crazy thing. Often the disc will wobble and then
plummet straight into the ground. At other times it will sail way
too high and come right back at the person launching it. You may
see where I'm headed with this illustration. The time period we're
discussing, ages eight to twelve, are like the motion when the Frisbee
thrower is just about to release the disc, but has not yet done so.

In preparation for release, the Frisbee goes out and back, being
extended just short of arm's length and coiled back in. This is what
our tweens are experiencing. They feel both closeness and distance
in their relationship with us. They believe they should stay close by
our sides, and yet they know they need to venture out and explore
as well.

This hard work may, of course, become extremely frustrating over
time. Remember, parenting well isn't hard—it's almost *impossible*.
That's why we need the supernatural power of God to intercede

on our behalf. We need the Holy Spirit to work in the areas where we lack the skill or insight to parent effectively. And we need God to correct the mistakes we make. This is why parenting is a faith endeavor.

As engaged parents, we can easily become discouraged and believe much of our time is being wasted. We see few results or little progress being made. We need to ask God for the faith to believe that our efforts are worth the energy and time we're investing. I believe God smiles upon us when He sees us parenting with love, grace, and discipline.

The Spirit of Elijah

At the root of authentic communication with our tweens is the concept of union. When we make a heartfelt effort to reach our tweens—to connect—we are, in essence, bonding with them, and they are more readily open to the beliefs and values we work at passing along.

The Old Testament prophet Malachi closed his message to Israel with this warning from the Lord: "Behold, I am going to send you Elijah the prophet before the coming of the great and terrible day of the LORD. And he will restore the hearts of the fathers to their children, and the hearts of the children to their fathers, lest I come and smite the land with a curse" (Mal. 4:5–6).

Another word for restoration is reuniting. What a wonderful picture of God working in the hearts of his people and healing the land. Parents and tweens connecting in authentic communication is a necessary first step in the process of family, community, and national renewal. Visualize a community where parents and tweens have united or reunited! Parenting your tween well by using balance and authenticity is an important step in building a healthy community and a healthy country.

Advice from the "Trenches"

Some of the most memorable pieces of advice I've ever received have come not from the experts, but from folks who have been through what I'm going through. So I'd like to close the advice part of this book with the words of others in the trenches.

This first group of thoughts is from tweens and teens themselves. I asked them what advice they'd give parents and here's what they said:

> Raise us with care and funniness. Handle tough times through words not violence. I think that if you use words it will be less violent.
>
> —H. C., age 9

> Raise my allowance.
>
> —P. W., age 10

> Tell them right from wrong.
>
> —C. W. C., age 10

> They shouldn't rush kids in the morning.
>
> —A. B., age 10

> Please stop hassling me.
>
> —A. P. P., age 10

> Never take my advice.
>
> —T. R., age 10

> Don't yell.
>
> —E. M. P., age 10

> The more they ground us the less time we are happy, and I think that is why some teens are always sad or mad. So you can ground us but don't do it too much.
>
> —H. L., age 11

I think parents should listen to the kid's side of the story.

—E. K., age 11

Talk to them about drugs.

—E. T., age 11

Spend more time with your kids. [My mom] doesn't spend enough time with me.

—M. G., age 11

I think parents should be able to let their children tell them how they feel about the way parents treat them.

—B. D., age 12

Don't yell at kids. Spend more time with them. Give them chances to talk and be equal with your kids.

—N. S., age 12

To the parents I would tell them that giving advice to your child and doing it well is not so easy. So make sure you think out your advice. Hasty judgments and advice can give a nasty effect on your child.

—D. J. Z., age 13

I say that my parents don't need to shout and scream every word to me. They think that if they don't scream I won't do what they told me to. But I can hear them just fine. They could just talk normal to me. I am a teenager, not deaf.

—M. L., age 14

Don't spoil them and don't buy into the whole "no physical punishment" thing. Sometimes it's the only way to get through.

—J. P., age 15

Be involved in your kids' lives, but don't be nosy either.

—A. T., age 15

Encourage your kids to participate in any activities they are interested in.

—S. C., age 15

Don't make assumptions quickly.

—C. B., age 16

Don't jump to conclusions. Allow your child to tell you their story.

—J. S., age 16

Do your best to keep kids active and exercising.

—J. Z., age 17

The second batch of advice is from fellow parents. I asked them, "What advice would you give to parents who have children who are eight to twelve years old?" Here's what they said:

You don't always have to be your child's best friend. Be the authority and disciplinarian. Love them unconditionally, pray always that they will seek God's will.

—P. M., roofer

Develop a close relationship with your child while they are at this age, so that when they become teenagers you have a better opportunity of maintaining your relationship, closeness, and involvement in their lives and decisions when they reach the teenage years. Let them take on more responsibility and decisions as they mature.

—C. G., engineer

Guard their hearts as long as possible. Don't be afraid to say no!

—L. B., coach

As our Father is patient and kind to us, be the same to your tween.

—T. B., teacher

Get involved in their lives. Do things together that are fun for both them and you—see a Christian concert even if it hurts your ears! Join a church with a good youth group where they want to attend church. Don't take yourself too seriously. Make funny faces, make a fool of yourself. Create joyful memories.

—R. C., program
manager

Pay attention to the little things! The most insignificant action of yours will be the most profound memory of your child.

—D. R. H.,
telecom
director

Pick your battles. Try to say yes more than you say no.

—M. K. E.,
homemaker

Be involved! Watch the shows they watch and monitor the music they hear, know their teachers and friends!

> —S. M.,
> stay-at-home
> mom

Take time to talk with them about their interests and their friends. It's amazing what you can learn about what's going on in their lives. Then pray with them about the things you've talked about. A bond forms that is strong and consistent.

> —C. M., mother

- Imagine your children as adults.
- Treat your children how you would have wanted to be treated as a child.
- Introduce them to Jesus.
- Teach "mercy triumphs over judgment" (James 2:13).

> —R. W.,
> domestic
> engineer

Be involved in daily activities to monitor the influences of our world. Teach values—God first! Keep lines of communication open so they can express their views and ask questions.

> —T. D., doctor

Remember that your actions speak louder than your words. Kids at this age are having a real identity crisis trying to figure out where they fit in. Encourage them to find godly friends and try to know their friends as well as you can.

> —C. L., middle
> school teacher

You have to live the life you tell your kids to live; you can't drop them off at church. You have to be the example for the way your kids live their lives.

—A. L., sales

Help them to understand that just because other families (even Christian ones) do things a certain way or allow certain things does not mean that our family will do the same. The standard that we go by and that our daughter should go by is the standard Jesus Christ allowed.

—S. W.,
homemaker/
ranch manager

- Love unconditionally.
- Forgive your imperfections.
- Give quantity time.
- Spend quality time with your spouse.
- Never disrespect your wife/husband in front of the kids.
- Take lots of video and pictures.
- Praise your kids for positives.
- Help them memorize Scripture.

—R. T., software
developer

It is very tough in the world today to be different [from the majority] and to live a life pleasing to God. You may not see any rewards this side of heaven.

—S. W.,
engineer

Kids need boundaries. Do not be afraid to enforce your rules (even if their friends' parents' don't). Spend time with your children whenever you can. The little things can be what impact them most.

—L. C.,
pediatrician

I would advise parents to let their children understand it is okay to be different. They don't have to try to be like everyone else.

—G. M.,
customer
service

Don't negotiate with them. You make the decisions. They are the child; you are the adult. Always follow up with what you say. If you aren't going to do it—don't say it.

—J. J.

Always be prepared to listen, regardless of what important activity you may be involved in at the moment. Refrain from communicating from a premise of distrust. If a concern needs to be addressed, do so from a position of love and trust. Offer hugs and words of encouragement consistently.

—M. M.

One of the best things I've found with our nine-year-old boy is to talk with him about the decisions I make and why I make those decisions. He's at a point where he's making many of his own decisions now, and seeing how we use God's Word to help make adult decisions helps him to apply God's Word to how he is going to live his life.

—M. J., business
analyst

Deuteronomy 6:7. I have realized that parenting is between God, my husband, and me. My parenting skills are not open for popular public opinion, or pressure from others.

—C. S.,
self-employed

The greatest reward is hearing my child at a young age remind me when I say, "I love you more than anyone in the world." Then my child responds, "No, remember Mom, we love Jesus most of all."

—C. B. J.,
homemaker

If you want to have a positive influence on your kids, then you need to positively influence your kids' friends.

—P. W., general
manager

Teach them to save. Saving money from recycled aluminum cans has added up to over two thousand dollars in fifteen years for our son. Little amounts along the way really add up. With money, teach responsibility. For example, have a percent to save, a percent to spend, and a percent given to charity.

—J. M., training
director

Listen to your kids. Plan activities that meet their desires and broaden their horizons. Listening develops a relationship with the child and builds trust that you care for/love them.

—B. T. S.,
software
engineer

Chapter Review

- Practicing authentic communication requires spending both quality and quantity time with your tween.

- One of the blocks to speaking with authenticity and vulnerability with our children may come from our own fears or doubts about parenting. It's important to overcome those and be honest with our children.

- One of the reasons it's so important to practice authentic communication with our tweens is because they long to connect with us and desire a heart-to-heart relationship with a caring adult. If they don't experience this type of relationship with us, they will seek it elsewhere.

- Authentic communication takes practice and skill. Talk with your children often. Turn off electronic devices and look into your child's eyes. Practice speaking from your heart.

Chapter Discussion Questions

1. Why is it important to spend both quality and quantity time with your tween?

2. Describe a recent time when you felt you and your tween had a heart-to-heart conversation. What specifically happened to move the conversation along?

3. Why does listening to our tweens require humility? How do you feel when you are trying to communicate with someone and you sense she's not really listening?

4. What electronic modes of communicating do your tweens employ that you know little about? Is communicating digitally or electronically the same as talking face-to-face? Why or why not?

7

Case Studies and Discussion Questions

Throughout, this book has presented basic ideas, concepts, and thoughts on raising your tween. There are even some examples and how-to's. But there's nothing quite like practice.

So in this section are included several case studies for you to practice. Case studies are real-life scenarios where you, your spouse, and even your children can discuss and struggle with concepts in order to bring out differing ideas regarding the topic at hand. The purpose of a case study is not to come to a right or wrong answer regarding the problem. Rather, the discussion itself is the purpose, and the issues raised should help additional questions surface and spark further insights into one's own particular set of circumstances. In each of these case studies the tween serves as the main subject.

Case Study 1

Perceived Problem

Eight-year-old Brooke is a self-professed tomboy who likes to compete with her older brother, Steve. Her mom, Michelle, is worried about Brooke's "masculine tendencies," and wishes she would spend more time with the other girls in her class. Michelle wants her daughter to wear pretty dresses, go shopping with her at the mall, and learn how to bake. Brooke says she hates wearing dresses and sees nothing wrong with her baggy jeans and athletic sweatshirts.

143

Brooke's dad, Phil, on the other hand, keeps telling his wife that Brooke is just going through a phase and that she's perfectly normal. Phil takes Steve and Brooke to football games, and they both love it. The three of them recently went on a hunting trip, and everyone had a great time. Phil says it's not right to force Brooke to wear a dress if she doesn't feel comfortable.

Proposed Solution

Michelle has proposed using a balanced-parenting practice. During family discussion time at the dinner table she announces her idea. Michelle believes that for every hunting trip or sporting event Brooke attends with her dad, Michelle ought to be able to spend time with Brooke, participating in "girls' night out" activities. She also proposes that the family go on more outings that everyone can enjoy.

Group Discussion Questions

1. Are Michelle's worries about her daughter's gender development a legitimate concern? How could Michelle use authentic communication with Brooke?

2. If Phil is right and Brooke is just going through a phase, does it matter whether Brooke ever wears a dress? Do styles of clothing even matter today?

3. Is Michelle right to ask for equal time regarding events and activities with Brooke? What if Brooke really doesn't want to spend time with her mom?

4. Phil keeps insisting that, because Brooke is only eight years old, she has plenty of time to develop into a feminine woman. Michelle is not convinced. What should this family do? What other issues could be underlying this potential conflict?

Case Study 2

Perceived Problem

Although it's been close to a year since his mom's second marriage, ten-year-old Jonathan has never really bonded with his new stepdad, Mike. Jonathan keeps demanding he be allowed to spend more time with his biological dad, Craig. Jonathan's mom, Tricia, prefers that Jonathan not see Craig so often because she doesn't approve of her ex-husband's temper and his choice in music and movies. She says her son would really love Mike the way she does if Jonathan would only spend more time with him and get to know him better.

Tricia tries to talk with Jonathan to see why he wants to see his dad so often, but Jonathan clams up and keeps his feelings inside. She's noticed Jonathan's angry outbursts lately but doesn't know the best way to help her son.

Proposed Solution

Mike wants to use a balanced-parenting tip. He asks that the family set up a visitation calendar on which trips to Craig's are clearly outlined and scheduled in advance. Mike believes if Jonathan knows ahead of time when he could expect to see his dad, their own relationship might improve over time. Tricia agrees to this idea but also wants Jonathan and Mike to sit down and talk on a regular basis so they can develop a healthy relationship.

Group Discussion Questions

1. Why do you think Jonathan wants to see his biological father so often? As a ten-year-old, should he also be expected to bond with his stepdad, Mike, or is Tricia harboring unrealistic expectations?

2. How can Tricia help her son develop a healthy self-identity? Does the reason for their divorce factor into this equation? What about the character of her ex-husband, Craig? Does that matter in this particular family system?

3. Mike wants to have authentic conversations with his stepson, Jonathan. How can he connect at a heart-to-heart level? What communication strategies should Mike try? How can Mike overcome some of the blocks that Jonathan puts up?

4. Is Tricia's proposal that Jonathan and Mike sit down and talk on a regular basis a realistic one?

5. Since Jonathan is only ten years old, does he really have the right to demand to see his biological father? Why or why not?

6. What potential problems or successes do you foresee for this family over the long term? Discuss this family's future and describe several possible scenarios.

Case Study 3

Perceived Problem

Nine-year-old Emily and twelve-year-old Madison are fairly well-adjusted sisters who get along nicely. They are being raised by their hardworking, single mom, Valerie. There is no father involvement in this family system. Madison could best be described as an overachiever while Emily has been labeled an underperformer. The problem this family struggles with is Valerie's continual comparing of her two daughters. When Valerie compares Madison and Emily, Emily always comes out on the short end of the stick. And while Valerie never states the words explicitly, the message Emily keeps receiving is, *Why can't you be more like your sister?* When Emily feels the comparisons coming she becomes depressed and retreats to her bedroom.

Proposed Solution

At Emily's request, the family has agreed to sit with the school guidance counselor to receive advice. The counselor urges Valerie to try and focus on the strengths and weaknesses of both of her daughters. The counselor also encourages Valerie to learn to be open to discussions with Emily when Emily feels she's being compared to Madison. Future meetings are set up for the first Tuesday evening of each month so the counselor can check on the progress of this family.

Group Discussion Questions

1. Valerie thought comparing the shortcomings of her younger daughter with the strengths of her older daughter might help Emily see how much potential she possesses. Is this a healthy communication strategy? Why or why not?

2. When Emily becomes depressed she retreats to her bedroom and turns up the volume on her stereo. Should Valerie follow her into the bedroom or allow her to have her "alone time"? Should Madison step in and try to talk with her sister?

3. Because there seems to be no one else to talk with, this family decided to visit the school guidance counselor. Did the guidance counselor give healthy advice? What advice would you give this family if they came to visit you? Be specific.

4. Research shows that if no father is present in a family, it is healthy for children to be involved with a caring father figure. Where would this family go to find healthy male involvement in their family? Do you agree a father figure is needed? What difference would a father presence make in this family?

Case Study 4

Perceived Problem

Like most boys his age, eleven-year-old Justin enjoys trading baseball cards, playing board games, and chatting with his friends online. Lately, however, his online activities have become a near obsession. His parents, Chuck and Jean, have discussed limiting Justin's Internet involvement. Justin's eight-year-old sister, Christie, used to play her favorite computer game, "Falling Snowflakes," after Justin was finished using the Internet. But lately, Justin just continues online chatting with his friends and never allows Christie to come near the family computer. For his birthday, Justin has asked for his own laptop computer so he can browse the Internet from the privacy of his bedroom. Christie thinks this is a great idea, but Justin's parents are not convinced.

Proposed Solution

Jean stops her son's youth pastor in the hallway at church to inquire about her son's online activities. The youth pastor agrees that all the kids are chatting online these days, but goes on to tell how most parents in the church are now limiting their children's Internet usage to a certain amount of time each day. He also mentions how some parents are setting up trade-offs: for each block of time the tween is on the computer the child is required to spend an equal amount of time performing chores or completing homework assignments. Christie hears the plan and believes it is a fair one, which will allow her to play "Falling Snowflakes" more often. Justin hears the plan and announces this new family rule stinks.

Group Discussion Questions

1. Is Justin's constant online computer usage a problem or is this family overreacting? Some families in this church don't allow their tweens to be online at any time. Is there a balanced-parenting approach to Internet usage?

2. Chuck wants to spend more time engaged in authentic communication with his son, Justin. But Justin says he would rather engage in online chat with his friends because it's so fun and unpredictable. In addition, when he and his dad talk, Justin says it always ends up being more of a lecture than a discussion. What can Chuck do?

3. Chuck is concerned that if Christie ends up in the family room playing "Falling Snowflakes" and his son is in his bedroom chatting online on his laptop, that the family will spend even less time together than they do now. Should Chuck be concerned or is he just a product of an earlier age when electronic devices were scarce?

4. Jean wants her son to attend youth group at their church. Justin argues that, in a sense, he is spending as much time or more with the kids in the youth group because they all chat

with him online. Jean says there's a big difference between going to church and chatting online, that sitting at a keyboard staring at a screen is just not the same as interacting with kids during the church youth programs. Discuss these specific family dynamics and offer helpful solutions to these difficult issues.

Notes

Introduction: Where Did My Child's Childhood Go?

1. *Wikipedia: The Free Encyclopedia*, s.v. "puberty," http://en.wikipedia.org/wiki/Puberty (accessed on June 30, 2005).

2. *Wikipedia: The Free Encyclopedia*, s.v. "adolescence," http://en.wikipedia.org/wiki/Adolescence (accessed on June 30, 2005).

3. J. M. Tanner and P. S. Davies, "Clinical Longitudinal Standards for Height and Weight Velocity for North American Children," *Journal of Pediatrics* 107 (1985): 317–29.

4. Cynthia Jones Neal, "A Parental Style for Nurturing Christian Wisdom," in *Limning the Psyche: Explorations in Christian Psychology,* ed. Robert C. Roberts and Mark R. Talbot (Grand Rapids: Eerdmans, 1997), 172.

5. Tim Kimmel, *Grace-Based Parenting: Set Your Family Free* (Nashville: W Publishing Group, 2004), 20.

6. Lisa Hutchinson Wallace and David C. May, "The Impact of Parental Attachment and Feelings of Isolation on Adolescent Fear of Crime at School," *Adolescence* 40.159 (Fall 2005), 460.

Chapter 1: The Need for Balanced Parenting

1. J. Allen and D. Land, "Attachment in Adolescence," in *Handbook of Attachment,* ed. J. Cassidy and P. Shaver (New York: Guilford, 1999), 319–35.

2. Nancy E. Sherwood, "Girls Can Internalize Negative Body Images Even as Pre-adolescents," *American Journal of Health*

Promotion, March 2001, http://www.eurekalert.org (accessed June 30, 2005).

3. R. H. Rubin, K. H. Dwyer et al. "Attachment, Friendship, and Psychosocial Functioning in Early Adolescence," *Journal of Early Adolescence* 24.4 (November 2004): 333.

4. E. Olcay Imamoglu, "Individuation and Relatedness: Not Opposing but Distinct and Complementary," *Genetic, Social, and General Psychology Monographs* 129.4 (November 2003): 370.

5. Joseph Nicolosi and Linda Ames Nicolosi, *A Parent's Guide to Preventing Homosexuality* (Downers Grove, IL: InterVarsity Press, 2002), 22.

6. American Psychiatric Association, *Diagnostic and Statistical Manual of Mental Disorders,* 4th ed. (Washington, DC: American Psychiatric Assoc., 1994), 581.

7. Sylvia B. Rimm, "Preserving Middle Childhood for the 'T Generation,'" *Principal,* September–October 2006, 27. This material originally appeared in Rimm's book, *Growing Up Too Fast: The Rimm Report on the Secret World of America's Middle Schoolers* (Emmaus, PA: Rodale, 2005).

8. When Jesus became separated from his parents in the temple crowd, his parents felt comfortable enough to leave with the caravan without him by their side, assuming he was "among their relatives and friends" (Luke 2:44 NIV).

9. According to the Mishnah, a Jewish boy became responsible for his religious commitments at the age of thirteen.

10. See Mark 12:30.

11. YMCA, "A Brief History of the YMCA Movement," www.ymca.net.

12. 4-H, "Frequently Asked Questions," www.4husa.org.

13. United States Department of Health and Human Services, "Verb: It's What You Do: Media Campaign to Increase Positive Physical and Social Behavior Among the Nation's Youth," Press Release, July 17, 2002, http://www.hhs.gov/news (accessed June 30, 2005).

14. Tony D. Crespi, "Children of Alcoholics and Adolescence: Individuation, Development, and Family Systems," *Adolescence*, Summer 1997, http://www.findarticles.com/p/articles/mi_m2248/is_n126_v32/ai19619421/print (accessed September 9, 2004).

15. James McBreen, quoted in *University of Cincinnati E-Briefs*, July 21, 2000, http://www.uc.edu/news/ebriefs/tween.htm (accessed June 30, 2005). McBreen is an adjunct professor of social work, University of Cincinnati, Cincinnati, OH.

16. Søren Kierkegaard, *Papers and Journals: A Selection*, trans. Alastair Hannay (London: Penguin Books, 1996), 295.

17. Anne Ortlund, *Children Are Wet Cement* (Old Tappan, NJ: Revell, 1981), 38–40.

18. M. K. Freitag, J. Belsky, K. Grossman, J. E. Grossman, and H. Scheurer-Englisch, "Continuity in Child-Parent Relationships from Infancy to Middle Childhood and Relations with Friendship Competence," *Child Development* 67 (1996): 1437–54.

19. R. H. Rubin, K. H. Dwyer et al., "Attachment, Friendship, and Psychosocial Functioning in Early Adolescence," *Journal of Early Adolescence* 24.4 (November 2004): 329.

20. Institute for American Values, *Hardwired to Connect: The New Scientific Case for Authoritative Communities* (New York: Institute for American Values, 2003).

21. Mark Crispen Miller, "The Merchants of Cool" (2000). A 1999 study conducted by the U.S. Center for Media Education.

22. "National Study of Youth and Religion" (Chapel Hill: University of North Carolina, 1997). A national longitudinal survey of youth.

Chapter 2: Preparing Your Tween to Leave the Nest

1. Dawn M. Upchurch, Carol S. Aneshensel, Clea A. Sucoff, and Lene Levy-Storms, "Neighborhood and Family Contexts of Adolescent Sexual Activity," *Journal of Marriage and the Family* 61 (November 1999): 920–33.

2. News.com.au, "Children 'Addicted from First Puff,'" *Sunday Telegraph* 2006, http://www.news.com.au/story/0,23599,20380684-36398,00.html (accessed September 9, 2006).

3. Nick and Nancy Stinnett, and Joe and Alice Beam, *Fantastic Families: 6 Proven Steps to Building a Strong Family* (West Monroe, LA: Howard Publishing, 1999), 10.

4. Media Awareness Network, "Special Issues for Tweens and Teens," http://www.media-awareness.ca/english/parents/marketing/issues_teens_marketing.cfm (accessed June 30, 2005).

5. A. Angyal, "A Theoretical Model for Personality Studies," *Journal of Personality* 20 (1951): 140.

6. Mahasin F. Saleh, Ruth S. Buzi, Maxine L. Weinman, and Peggy B. Smith, "The Nature of Connections: Young Fathers and Their Children," *Adolescence* 40.159 (Fall 2005): 519.

7. James Dobson, *Parenting Isn't for Cowards* (Dallas: Word, 1987), 145.

8. Mike Langberg, "Cell Phone Training Wheels for Tweens," *San Francisco Mercury News,* June 27, 2005.

Chapter 3: When You Overcontrol Your Tween

1. Ken Canfield, *The 7 Secrets of Effective Fathers* (Wheaton, IL: Tyndale House, 1992), 58.

2. Andrew Stern, "TV Is Bad for Children's Education, Studies Say," *Archives of Pediatrics and Adolescent Medicine,* July 4, 2005, Reuters News Agency. Study author: Dina Borzekowski of Johns Hopkins University, Baltimore, MD.

3. Ross Campbell, *Relational Parenting* (Chicago: Moody, 2000), 15.

4. Gary Chapman, *Five Signs of a Functional Family* (Chicago: Northfield Publishing, 1997).

5. Charles R. Swindoll, *You and Your Child* (Nashville: Thomas Nelson, 1977), 150.

6. "The Unilever/Girl Scout Self-Esteem Survey," conducted by RoperASW, a national survey of more than 800 preteens, ages 8–12, cited in "Worries About Academics, Making Parents Proud: Top Concerns for 'Tweens,'" *Market Wire,* September 17, 2003, http://www.couplescompany.com/wireservice/ Parenting/TweenJitters.htm.

7. Jeffrey A. Dvorkin, *Crime Reporting: Too Much for Listeners?* http://www.NPR.org (July 6, 2005).

Chapter 4: When You Undercontrol Your Tween

1. Seth J. Schwartz, Hilda Pantin, Guillermo Prado, Summer Sullivan, and Jose Szapocznik, "Family Functioning, Identity, and Problem Behavior in Hispanic Immigrant Early Adolescents," *Journal of Early Adolescence* 25.4 (November 2005): 392–420.

2. Linda Berg-Cross, *Basic Concepts in Family Therapy: An Introductory Text,* 2d ed. (New York: Haworth Press, 2000), 53.

3. Terril Yue Jones, "24/7, Teens Get the Message," *Los Angeles Times,* June 23, 2005, http://www.latimes.com/ (accessed June 30, 2005).

4. Jane Buckingham, quoted in Bella English, "The Disappearing Tween Years," *Boston Globe,* March 12, 2005, http://www

.boston.com/ (accessed July 6, 2005). Jane Buckingham is president of Youth Intelligence.

5. Associated Press, "Sex Offender-Free Subdivision Offered— Builders in Lubbock Give Guarantee, Promise Background Checks," *Dallas Morning News* shared content, http://www .WFAA.com/ (accessed June 6, 2005).

6. Kenneth and Elizabeth Gangel, *Building a Christian Family: A Guide for Parents* (Chicago: Moody, 1987), 52.

7. J. Snarey, *How Fathers Care for the Next Generation: A Four-Decade Study* (Cambridge, MA: Harvard University Press, 1993), cited in *Father Facts*, by Wade F. Horn and Tom Sylvester, 4th ed. (Gaithersburg, MD: National Fatherhood Initiative, 2002), 102.

8. United States Department of Health and Human Services, "Verb: It's What You Do: Media Campaign to Increase Positive Physical and Social Behavior Among the Nation's Youth," Press Release, July 17, 2002, http://www.hhs.gov/news (accessed June 30, 2005).

9. Quoted in Bella English, "The Disappearing Tween Years: Bombarded by Sexualized Cultural Forces, Girls Are Growing Up Faster Than Ever," *The Boston Globe*, http://www .boston.com (March 12, 2005).

Chapter 5: Why Authentic Communication with Your Tween Is Critical

1. J. Mosely and E. Thompson, "Fathering Behavior and Child Outcomes: The Roles of Race and Poverty," in *Fatherhood: Contemporary Theory, Research and Social Policy*, ed. W. Marsiglio (Thousand Oaks, CA: Sage Publications, 1995), 148–65.

2. National Mental Health Association, www.nmha.org (accessed June 5, 2005).

3. Henry Cloud and John Townsend, *Boundaries: When to Say Yes, When to Say No, to Take Control of Your Life* (Grand Rapids: Zondervan, 1992), 41.

4. James Dobson, *The New Dare to Discipline* (Wheaton, IL: Tyndale House 1996), 36.

5. Paul A. Paterson, "Tweens Take Over: Y Generation Is the Wunderkind of Brand Marketing," *TD Monthly* 2.6 (June 2003) http://www.toydirectory.com/monthly/June2003/ Tweens_Generations.asp (accessed June 30, 2005).

6. Charles R. Swindoll, *The Strong Family* (Plano, TX: Insight for Living, 1997), 31.

7. Dan Wheeler, quoted in *University of Cincinnati E-Briefs*, July 21, 2000, http://www.uc.edu/news/ebriefs/tween.htm (accessed June 30, 2005). Wheeler is an associate professor of education, University of Cincinnati, Cincinnati, OH.

8. Anne R. Rice and David Evans, "Staples/Boys and Girls Clubs of America," *USA Today Snapshots* interactive media, June 2005.

Chapter 6: Using Authentic Communication to Tune In to Your Tween

1. Ronald B. Adler and Neil Towne, *Looking Out, Looking In*, 10th ed. (Belmont, CA: Wadsworth/Thomson Learning, 2003), 67.

2. Ronald Levant, as cited by Laura Shapiro and Claudia Kalb, "The Myth of Quality Time," *Newsweek* 129.19 (May 12, 1997): 62.

3. Kevin Leman, *Making Children Mind Without Losing Yours* (Old Tappan, NJ: Revell, 1984), 30.

4. Philips Consumer Communications, "Let's Connect," Philips National Family Communication Survey of 5th–8th Graders and Their Parents, 1998. Cited from The Center for

Parent/Youth Understanding Web site, 2003, http://cpyu.org/ Page–paspx?id=76972 (accessed September 18, 2006).

5. Gary Smalley and John Trent, *The Blessing* (Nashville: Thomas Nelson, 1986), 27.

6. Eric I. Knudsen, "Sensitive Periods in the Development of Brain and Behavior," *Journal of Cognitive Neuroscience* 16 (October 2004): 1412–25.

For information on scheduling a workshop, seminar, or retreat, contact:

Dynamic Dads
P.O. Box 140369
Dallas, Texas 75214

A Guide to Everything
a Dad Needs to Know

First-time dads-to-be have plenty of questions about stepping into the shoes of a parent, but few guys want to sit down for "baby talk" with their friends. So where can a dad get the information he needs? This is the resource to turn to. Set up in an easy-to-follow A-to-Z format, *Congratulations You're Gonna Be a Dad!* offers sound advice from veteran father Paul Pettit and his wife, Pam—who gives dads a female perspective, as well as insights from her medical training. Along for the ride are several other "seasoned dads," including James Dobson and Chuck Swindoll, to pass along their experiences of the ups and downs of fatherhood.

"Here's a book that will help first-time dads get off to a good start."

—Dr. Joseph M. Stowell
President, Moody Bible Institute

12/22